W9-AAV-977

Barbara A. Ganim

How to Approach an Advertising Agency and Walk Away With the Job You Want

VGM Career Horizons
a division of *NTC Publishing Group*
Lincolnwood, Illinois USA

**HALF HOLLOW HILLS
COMMUNITY LIBRARY**

Library of Congress Cataloging-in-Publication Data

Ganim, Barbara.
   How to approach an advertising agency and walk away with the job
you want / Barbara A. Ganim
      p.   cm.
   Includes bibliographical references and index.
   ISBN 0-8442-3525-3
   1. Advertising—Vocational guidance.   I. Title.
HF5828.4.G36 1993
659. 1'023'73—dc20   92-38028
                                                                  CIP

Published by VGM Career Horizons, a division of NTC Publishing Group
4255 West Touhy Avenue, Lincolnwood (Chicago), Illinois 60646-1975, U.S.A.
© 1993 by Barbara A. Ganim. All rights reserved.
No part of this book may be reproduced, stored in a retrieval system,
or transmitted in any form or by any means,
electronic, mechanical, photocopying, recording or otherwise,
without the prior permission of NTC Publishing Group.
Manufactured in the United States of America.

3 4 5 6 7 8 9 BC 9 8 7 6 5 4 3 2 1

To Susan Fox, without you this book would never have been written.

CONTENTS

STEP TWO

Choose an area of specialization 29

STEP THREE

Focus in on the niche   41

STEP FOUR

Select the agencies that are right for you   68

STEP FIVE

Give the agency what it is looking for   80

STEP SIX

Put together a personal presentation package 93

STEP SEVEN

Make your move 128

STEP EIGHT

Keep the job once you get it 145

Advertising— what's the attraction?

Back when I was just beginning to dabble in "advertising," I thought the very word hung magically in the air just waiting for me to reach up and grab it. You should know that I knew next to nothing about my then favorite word. Although I was running my own small graphic design business and teaching design and illustration at a local college, advertising as a profession was something I only dreamed about. The word "advertising" conjured up an image of Madison Avenue, high tech graphics, and slick, four-color layouts in *Newsweek, Time* and *Gentlemen's Quarterly*. I imagined that producing television commercials was just as far outside my realm of possibility as orchestrating multi-million dollar Hollywood extravaganzas. And I truly believed that all advertising executives drove Mercedes and Porsches, took two hour lunches to wine and dine corporate CEOs, and lived in a non-stop frenzy of creative inspiration.

Was I caught up in the glamorous fantasy world popularized by racy novels, prime-time soaps, and sitcoms? Yes! Was I misinformed? Absolutely! It would take two years for this naive impression to be replaced by the reality of a career in advertising. But the fantasy served its purpose. It captured my imagination, gave me something to aim for, and kept me going.

My entrance into the real world of advertising began when a series of innocent events started a chain reaction that changed my life. As my small design business began to grow, I read and studied everything I could about advertising theory, writing copy, marketing strategies, and media production. Then one day the Dean of Continuing Education at the college where I was still teaching part-time asked if I would like to handle the advertising account for her division. There was no doubt in my mind that I was ready. The next day I officially added the word "advertising" to the name of my graphic design business and was on my way.

That was over twelve years ago. Changing the name of my business to include advertising was the easy part. The hard part was finding out that advertising involved much more than writing copy or media production. Advertising is about understanding what people want and determining how to give it to them. Looking back on my experience as a graphic designer turned agency owner, I have had the opportunity to learn how that same understanding applies to getting a job in advertising. That, too, is about knowing what an employer wants and how to provide it. I can see why some people are successful in finding jobs and others are not.

In order to share what I have learned, I've developed eight steps that will prepare you to approach the agencies of your choice and get the job you want. In *Step One* you will explore your own work environment and job structure preferences, examine your personal and work-related values, and articulate your needs and attitudes toward money. You'll learn how to evaluate what you already have in the way of personal experiences, education, and training that will qualify you for the job of your dreams in advertising. *Step Two* will help you choose an area of specialization. *Step Three* will show you how to evaluate your ability to fit into the areas of specialization you have selected. In *Step 4* you'll see how to match your skills and interests with the agencies you want to approach. *Step Five* will give you the information you need to sell yourself to the agencies that are right for you. *Step Six* will prepare you to put together your own personal presentation package that includes a cover letter to grab the attention of any agency president and a resume that best demonstrates your capabilities. *Step Seven* will show you how to make your move to approach the agencies of your choice through networking with family, friends, and professional contacts inside and outside the advertising community. If you have done your homework and prepared yourself well but the job you want is just not available, you also will discover how to make an offer a potential employer cannot refuse. In *Step Eight* you will learn about the unspoken expectations that lurk in the minds of every employer and how these expectations can be met without sacrificing your own personal values. You will also learn how to recognize and avoid the traps that keep most people running in place when they could be moving ahead.

My methods to help you prepare to get that job in advertising will involve a lot more preparation than most people ever do before their resumes hit the post office. But they will save you the trial and error uncertainty that can defeat you before you have really had a fair chance.

There is no way around it, advertising is a very exciting and often glamorous profession. If you have to work for a living, and most of us do, where else can you find a job that will challenge your creativity, your ability to think fast on your feet, and keep you moving at a rapid fire pace every single day? Where else will you get the opportunity to work with some of the best actors, voice talents, photographers, videographers, writers, and artists in the country? And where, but in advertising, can you jump up, in front of more than fifty corporate executives in a conference room the size of a football field, and make a presentation in which you sing a silly jingle and usher in a trio of jugglers to demonstrate what the company's next TV commercial will look like?

I've been in love with advertising over the years, and I've had my moments of hating it. The pressure is constant! The competition is fierce. But I must confess that some of the most exciting things I've ever done in my life did involve advertising.

If you think that your passion is in advertising, then get ready. When you finally get the job that you want, you'll be in for the time of your life. It won't always be easy, but it will definitely be exciting.

INTRODUCTION

What are agencies looking for in a prospective employee?

While it is true that agency principals (owners) are interested in hiring talented, creative people with solid training from reputable schools, the single most important factor they look for is whether this person can make an immediate and ongoing contribution to the operation of their business. Will this person's work support the salary and benefits the agency will have to pay? The new employee must be able to come into the agency on Day One with little or no supervision and begin to do work that is billable. Billable work is anything done for a client that can be billed directly to that client. If someone in the agency has to train a new employee, the new employee will be a liability to the agency, and the "trainer" will not be clocking in billable hours, either. So even if someone has plenty of talent, a string of impressive degrees, and an eye-popping portfolio, it does not mean that that person has the qualifications that can be readily utilized by an agency.

So, you may be saying to yourself, "Then how am I going to get a job in an agency if I've never worked in an agency and have no practical experience to offer?" That, of course, is the age old rub—you need experience to get the job, and you need the job to get experience. But do not be discouraged. You will discover as you read this book that you in fact do have experiences that are valuable to an agency. While that experience may have nothing to do with advertising, it still can be applied to the ongoing, billable work of an agency. And it is that experience, not your overflowing creativity and talent, that will make you attractive to a potential employer.

For instance, you may be interested in finding a position as a graphic designer, but other than a portfolio filled with school projects, you have no actual experience in taking a real graphics job from start to finish. However, when you think back on your past employment experiences—summer jobs, etc.—you remember that you worked two summers and a full semester as a clerk in a clothing store. In that job you had to know about clothing—brand names, styles, and materials. You also had to understand what motivated people (your customers) to be attracted to and want to buy the various styles of clothing your store sold. You had to know how to approach the people who came into the store, to get them to talk with you and to tell you what they were looking for. Then you had to help them make their selections and encourage them, without being pushy, to make a final decision to purchase the clothing. You had to work cooperatively with other salespeople. You were even involved in taking inventory and placing orders with clothing suppliers to replenish stock. Now, how does that kind of experience apply to an ad agency?

Your background would be an asset to an agency because your experience with customers in sales would have prepared you to feel comfortable to call and meet with clients for pick-ups, deliveries, and approvals on art work during various stages of a project. This would save the account executives from having to do a lot of running around to meet with clients when their expertise was not really necessary. That would free them up to spend more time bringing in new business. Your inventory and record-keeping experience was great preparation for calling or meeting with printers, typesetters, and other vendors to get price quotes for projects, maintaining project files, keeping track of prices and expenses, and recording time sheet hours. Your design school training certainly prepared you to handle many different phases of a graphics project, such as preparing paste-ups and overlays, transferring rough layout sketches into more finished pieces of work, proofing boards and type, and so on. That work would free up more experienced people to do other billable work. While you were doing all of this, you would of course be closely watching people in the graphics department and making it your business to learn everything you could about taking a project to completion. When you were ready, you would begin to take on more responsibility in a project. In addition, if you were working for an agency that handled retail clothing-store accounts, you would be a valuable addition to the creative team because you would know about styles and trends, brand names, and what motivates customers to buy.

This example illustrates how any kind of experience, whether it is job- or school-related, is an excellent resource for transferable skills that can be put to immediate use by an agency. Even extracurricular activities like working on the school newspaper or yearbook or being a class officer can be an excellent source of employment preparation. You will find, as you look back on your own past with the help of the exercises in the upcoming chapters, that you will have numerous experiences to draw upon that can be applied to agency work. Once you identify that experience, you then need to communicate in a cover letter and again during an interview *what* and *how* it can be put to use by the agency. This would show them that if you were hired, you could hit the ground running.

How to avoid the job search mistakes most people make

What are the mistakes people make when looking for a job in advertising? Quite simply, they revolve around a lack of preparation on the job hunter's part and a failure to focus in clearly on the agency world. I have identified the six most common mistakes that I see repeatedly. These are, simply:

- Failing to target specific agencies
- Not knowing what *you* really want and which agency is best suited to you
- Not attracting enough interest with your resume and cover letter
- Not understanding how advertising *really* works
- Relying on want-ads
- Not being prepared for the interview

Failure to target

The first thing most people do when they begin looking for a job is to take the shotgun approach. Unlike other firearms which send out a single bullet, shotguns spew hundreds of tiny pellets that cover a broad area. Hunters who use shotguns believe they will have a better chance of hitting their target with a wide sweep of pellets than with a sole slug. Many job hunters, too, have adapted this theory, believing that if they mass produce their resume and cover letters and then send them to every agency within a selected geographical area they will increase their

MISTAKES CREATIVES MAKE

Creatives are those people in an agency who develop the ideas for ad campaigns and other projects. Quite often newcomers to the profession who are looking for creative positions such as designers and copywriters will make one or more of the following mistakes while interviewing.

Mistake #1

The most common mistake is overstocking a portfolio. When an interviewer is forced to look at every piece of work an applicant has ever produced it is both annoying and time consuming. To avoid this mistake, include only your best work and limit the number of pieces you take. Ten to fifteen pieces is a good average. Along these same lines, don't talk too much about each piece. It is best to simply show the work, explain the project in ten words or less, and then wait to answer questions. If none are asked, move on.

Mistake #2

Some applicants are so focused on becoming an agency creative that they refuse to consider an entry-level position. The people most prone to this mistake are recent graduates whose work was favored by their professors. Their work was usually far better than that of fellow classmates and, as a result, they came to believe that their abilities would receive the same accolades in the job market. They also believe that talent is the most important factor agencies want. But talent is only a small part of the odds of finding an available position. The reality is that people who take this approach actually decrease their opportunities.

The reason is that every agency is different—not only in size but also in the particular market niche or niches each agency focuses on, the client base, the agency's structure, and the philosophy by which the agency is run. When someone sends a generic cover letter to an agency, it is glaringly apparent to whomever has the unfortunate task of reading it that this person took absolutely no interest in researching the agency. Research is the most important part of developing an ad campaign. And most agency people I know agree that those individuals wanting to work in advertising who ignore the research phase of their very first ad campaign—the selling of themselves to an agency—will not be worth considering. If these people cannot take the time to market themselves, or do not know how to research each agency they want to target, or do not position their capabilities in a way that is compatible with the information their research reveals, they certainly will not be very good at doing it for clients. I once received a generic cover letter from a young lady who began her letter with *Dear Sir*. She did not even know that my agency was owned by a woman. You can probably imagine what I did with her letter and resume.

business of advertising. Agencies need people with experience and experience can only be acquired on the job. Most neophytes, regardless of the splashing display of talent in their portfolio, will be brought to do the jobs that the agency creatives don't have time for, such as paste-ups, layouts, proofing, cutting overlays, and other rote production work, as well as answering the phone, picking up, and delivering.

Mistake #3

Sometimes if an interviewer is impressed with an applicant but a full-time position is unavailable, the applicant will be offered the opportunity to do some freelance work or come into the agency part-time. Some would-be creatives absolutely refuse to consider anything other than a full-time position. By following such a narrowly defined career path, they are actually undermining their own future opportunities. Many of the people I have hired in my agency began as either part-time employees or freelancers who became so valuable I brought them in at the first opportunity. I know this to be the case at other agencies as well.

In fact, freelancing can be a very smart route to take if you are having difficulty finding the kind of agency position you want. Rather than giving up and looking for employment elsewhere, you can offer to do some freelance work for the agencies that interview you but have no openings. This gives you an opportunity to get to know the people at the agencies and the kind of work they do. You will see first hand which agencies you like working with and which ones you want to avoid. You may also surprise yourself and find that you are attracted to the freedom, not to mention the money that can be made, when one becomes an experienced freelancer.

Not knowing what you want

In addition to not targeting in on prospective employers, job hunters also fail to target in on what they really want to do and what their capabilities are. Without this, you cannot pick the agencies or type of advertising work that is best suited for you. You also need to determine the kind of job you want and whether or not it is compatible with your training, interests, and capabilities. You must also learn how to examine any personal values that may create conflicts in a work environment. Knowing this ahead of time will help you choose the job that is just right for you when the time comes to make a decision. The second part of your research will be focused on the kind of agencies that your personal evaluations reveal are best suited to you.

During an interview, an agency owner recognizes that the interviewee can clearly make an immediate contribution to the ongoing work in the agency, the final determining factor in deciding to hire this person is often the sense that *this is a perfect match.* Is this chemistry? Maybe, but more than likely, it is the growing awareness that the person about to be offered a job has a personality that is truly compatible not only with the duties and responsibilities of the job but also with the agency's staff, the clients, and the very structure and philosophy of the agency itself. While this notion that someone is a perfect match can sometimes come across simply during an interview, taking the time to research and go after *only* those agencies for which you *are* a perfect match is going to make you stand out noticeably from the crowd of competitors anxiously vying for the same job. You cannot avoid the competition, but you can avoid looking just like them.

Not grabbing attention with initial contact

In addition to blanketing every agency around with a generalized cover letter and a watered down, no punch resume, and failing to research and target the most personally compatible agencies, job seekers also make another mistake that can eliminate them from consideration before they have even had a chance to demonstrate their abilities during an interview. Agency people receive phone calls and letters constantly from people inquiring about possible job openings. The majority of these inquiries are automatically screened out by the secretary as not being worth a busy executive's time. Most people think that their calls may not be returned, but surely their letters and resumes will be brought to the attention of the appropriate person. Not so! If there is nothing in that letter to grab the interest of the first person who opens the envelope—usually the secretary—the letter will end up in the wastebasket.

Not understanding the business of advertising

I have already mentioned the necessity of taking the time to find out exactly to whom in the agency your letter should be addressed. Along with that you must clearly communicate that your research indicates some distinct areas of compatibility between you and the agency. Another critical area that many people fail to address during their first point of contact with an agency is an understanding of how agencies operate as a business. Later in the book I will prepare you with basics regarding agencies and clients, how an agency makes money, and how agencies grow. But that is only the ingredient list for your recipe. To really get cooking you will need to read, on a regular basis, any local or regional advertising trade publications that are available. Check with your public library to see if they carry these trade journals. If not, they can tell you which libraries do. Industry trade journals, as well as your local newspaper business section, will tune you into who's who and what's what on the local advertising scene. When you write a letter to an agency and you can relate your experience as applicable to a specific account or market niche that agency has, you can bet you will get the reader's attention.

Relying on want-ads

Keeping up with the local trade journals can also be your most direct source of possible job openings. Most publications feature articles or blurbs on those agencies who have added new accounts. A new account usually means that additional staff people may be necessary to service the account. When an agency needs to get new staff people on board, the person in charge of hiring will try to avoid placing a classified ad. Why? Because it takes too long to sift through the barrage of responses to find competent and qualified people. That is when the job hunter with an ear to the ground can move in to make a timely appearance.

Not preparing for the interview

And finally, the last of the common mistakes unaware job hunters will make include not preparing adequately for an interview. When applicants are not well prepared for specific interviews, they end up over-selling themselves instead of being more focused on what the agency needs, talking too much and listening too little, under-dressing or over-dressing for the interview, and not taking their careers seriously. Every one of these danger zones will be explored in this book.

Perform a personal evaluation

See where you fit

You are unique. You have your own personal style, a way of working that is most productive for you. You also have your own set of talents and skills, and finding just the right balance between your work environment and job structure will help them flourish. This balance can make the difference between your ultimate success or failure in advertising.

For example, some people are nine-to-fivers who definitely need structure and direction in their work day. Others prefer to be left alone and set their own pace. There are those who find working in an open office distracting, unlike others who love the camaraderie of close working quarters. The person who thrives in a small agency, wearing many different hats, would probably be miserable in a large agency where people are often hired to perform only one aspect of a job. Before you can begin your job search, it is important to understand exactly what circumstances will enable you to perform at your best. The *workshops* in this chapter are designed to help you explore and evaluate your personal preferences for a work environment and the job structure that is most comfortable for you. Following that, you will examine your needs for financial security and how that can impact your decision to take a job that is not in your long-term best interest.

If you are a recent graduate or have limited work experience, you will find this section can help you envision how you might feel in a variety of work situations that you may have never encountered before. If you are a seasoned worker with years of employment experience under your belt, this chapter will give you an opportunity to compare the preferences you know you have to some you have never experienced or thought about.

Getting to know what you really want and need in a job is your first step toward finding the position that is exactly right for you. Your future success will be largely dependent on your compatibility with the environment you will have to work in each day and the job functions you will be expected to perform.

Sit back and relax. Make sure you will not be disturbed for at least the next half hour. You will need a pencil with an eraser. Do not use a pen. I want you to feel free to go back and change your answers at any point during these exercises. You may find yourself re-evaluating the choices you initially thought were extremely important to you as you begin to compare them to the other options presented here.

WORKSHOP 1

Exploring your work environment preferences

The following "you" statements relate to your personal preferences for a work environment. As you read through these statements, think back to some specific jobs that you have had in the past. They could serve as a basis for comparison. Ask yourself how you would feel about each job description that is being presented in these statements if you were actually in that situation. Is it something that you would be comfortable with? And would you be able to perform at your best under this specific circumstance? For those of you who have had limited job experience, try to envision yourself in each situation. You may not know for sure how you would react, but trust your intuition to guide your responses.

Evaluate each statement by using the letters **A** through **D**:

[A] I would love it.
[B] It would be comfortable.
[C] It would be uncomfortable.
[D] I would hate it, and would not accept it.

   Select only one letter. Choose the letter that best describes your reaction to each statement. Then write it in the space provided.

___   1. You have your own private office.

___   2. You share an office with another person.

___   3. You have your own work space in an open office with many other people.

___   4. You work in an open office with shoulder-level dividers that block off your space.

___   5. You share your desk with a part-time employee who works in the evenings.

___   6. The atmosphere in your office is lively and often noisy.

___   7. Everyone in your office is friendly, but they keep to themselves personally.

___   8. You work with people who are open and form friendships with each other quickly.

___   9. Your co-workers are professionally cordial, but they share limited conversation at work.

___ 10. The people in your department expect you to socialize with them after work.

___ 11. Your boss maintains a warm but professional distance from all employees.

___ 12. Your boss tries to "buddy-up" with employees.

___ 13. Your boss is hard to approach but always fair in making judgments.

___ 14. You are expected to spend personal time socializing with your boss.

___ 15. You are expected to spend personal time socializing with your company's clients.

___ 16. Your boss frequently calls you at home to discuss work matters.

___ 17. Professional dress (suits, etc.) is required in your office.

___ 18. You can dress casually in your office, but professional dress is required for meetings.

___ 19. Most people in your company wear jeans and sneakers.

___ 20. You are expected to tidy up your work space daily.

___ 21. Your agency's office is located in a large metropolitan city.

___ 22. You have to commute at least a half hour one way into this city each day.

___ 23. Your agency's office is in a beautiful and quiet rural setting. To get there you do have to drive more than 45 minutes one way.

___ 24. While there are many deadlines in your agency, the average work pace is relaxed and casual.

___ 25. Your agency handles many high powered accounts. As a result, the atmosphere is always fast paced, high energy, and frenzied. This kind of daily pressure to perform rarely lets up.

___ 26. Your boss treats clients with disrespect. To your amazement, this person not only gets away with it, but the clients keep coming back for more.

___ 27. Your agency is heavy in accounts that include nuclear energy waste plants, military armament industries, and several companies who have been brought up on environmental charges. These are major accounts bringing in tremendous revenues that result in numerous bonuses for you and other employees.

___ 28. You are about to accept a well-paying position with an ad agency. You have just discovered that the agency principals make a regular habit of over-charging their clients and padding the bills. How do you feel about accepting the job now?

___ 29. You have been offered a position that includes not only a fantastic salary but an outstanding benefits package. The only stipulation is that you will have to travel at least 60 percent of the time, and you will be expected to put in 60 to 70 hours a week. How do you feel about accepting this job based on that criteria?

___ 30. The salary may not be great and the agency is small, but you will have a tremendous opportunity for creative expression and possibly even a partnership if the agency continues to do well. How do you feel about accepting a job with this company?

Go back through your responses. Do any of them surprise you? If so, ask yourself why. Maybe it is because you have never thought about some of these situations before. Or you could be finding that the things you thought were important about your work environment are no longer that significant.

The letter you used to evaluate your reactions gives you a clear indication of what your personal needs are when it comes to being happy and comfortable in your work environment. Each statement you labeled with an **A** describes one specific part of a work environment that would be ideal for you. Those statements you classified as **B**s represent aspects of a work environment that you are comfortable with. The statements that received **C**s are the situations that create a sense of discomfort. And those marked with **D**s define the work environment that does not suit you.

While you may never find a job that is ideal in every way, if you can find a position that offers you more **A**s and **B**s than **C**s and **D**s you will find that your ability to stay in that position and perform at your very best will be greatly enhanced. All too many people look at the big picture when they direct themselves toward a career in advertising. They want a job in a good—if not great—agency, and they want to be doing exciting work and getting paid well for it. What they forget to think about is the small picture:

- Do I like the office I will be working in?
- Do I fit in comfortably with the people there?
- Do I respect the philosophy of the agency principals and their attitudes toward clients?
- Will my skills and talents be nurtured and encouraged to develop more in a small agency or a large one?
- Am I comfortable with the social atmosphere in this agency?

These questions and more are extremely important because they will determine your ability to achieve long-term success in this job. As for salary, while it may be your number one priority when you are evaluating a job offer, most people discover that after a month or two in an uncomfortable environment, salary is now their least important concern.

Clarifying your work environment preferences

By setting up these condensed listings described below, you will not have to constantly flip back through this book to review your preferences. Plus, they will be more firmly imbedded in your mind when the time comes to remember them the most. That time will be when you are actually doing your agency reviews and job search and then evaluating a job offer. Having a clear picture of what you need to function at your best in a new job will help you to eliminate, right from the start, those agencies or positions that are not comfortable or suitable for you.

In this exercise, briefly list all of your **A** through **D** statements from Workshop 1 under the appropriate headings below (1 through 4). As you write down each statement, reduce it to as few words as possible. For example, under heading #1 where you will list all of your **A**s, try to simplify them to read something like this: *My own office; Casual dress, except for meetings; A friendly office, but people keep to themselves;* etc. Do the same with all of your **B, C,** and **D** statements under their headings.

1. An ideal work environment for me would include any of the following: (Briefly list all of your **A**s)

_____

_____

_____

_____

_____

_____

_____

_____

_____

_____

2. I am comfortable with a work environment that includes any of the following: (Briefly list all of your **B**s)

_____

_____

_____

_____

_____

_____

_____

_____

_____

_____

_____

3. I am uncomfortable but will accept a work environment that includes any of the following: (Briefly list all of your **C**s)

_____

_____

_____

_____

_____

_____

_____

_____

_____

4. I should avoid a work environment that includes any of the following: (Briefly list all of your **D**s)

_____

_____

_____

_____

_____

_____

_____

_____

_____

_____

You should pay close attention to the description listings you included in #4 above. They represent some of the elements in a work environment that are not *at all* suited to your basic needs—whether that involves your need for privacy, office camaraderie, or your personal relationship with your boss. Be aware that you will always be pressured in the working world to set aside your own needs to accommodate those of your employer. Of course there will indeed be times when you will have to compromise on something that is important to you or risk losing a job altogether. After all, advertising is an incredibly competitive field and there will always be someone just as qualified waiting to take your place. As a result, you will walk a fine line, and you will have to use your best judgment to determine when and where to cross that line. But a compromise should come only after serious thought about its ultimate influence on your job performance in the long run. If you are accommodating just to please an employer, it could be at the expense of your own future success. Because in a contrary environment it will not take long for frustration, stress, and finally apathy to set in.

WORKSHOP 3

Examining job structure preferences

A compatible job involves not only your preferences for a work environment but also the structure of your job responsibilities. Certain duties, expectations, and job functions that you are called upon to perform will make you feel comfortable and confident, while others will create anxiety and discomfort. It is important to learn to recognize both.

In this exercise, you will find another set of "you" statements describing a variety of job structures that you could encounter in a new position. Once again, evaluate how you would react in each situation by writing one of the letters from **A** to **D** in the space provided below. **[A] I would love it; [B] It would be comfortable; [C] It would be uncomfortable, but I'd accept it; [D] I would hate it, and would not accept it.**

____ 1. You are continually asked to change the elements of the project you are working on.

____ 2. You are able to work at a steady and predictable pace.

____ 3. You are given assignments that are clearly outlined.

____ 4. You have a boss who says, "Take the ball and run."

____ 5. You have a boss who says, "You make the decisions—if you're wrong, it's your head!"

____ 6. You always work under the pressure of tight deadlines.

____ 7. Occasionally, you have an important deadline to meet.

____ 8. You juggle many different projects during the day.

____ 9. You are able to work on one assignment to completion before beginning the next.

___ 10. Your work on each new assignment is expected to be superior to your last project.

___ 11. You are asked to verbally explain your approach to each project to other members of your creative team.

___ 12. You are responsible for only one aspect of a project—without concern for the big picture.

___ 13. You have full responsibility for an assignment from beginning to end.

___ 14. As the group leader on a project, you are responsible for other people's contributions.

___ 15. You are working on assignments that involve only your best skills.

___ 16. You are working on an assignment that involves something you never did before.

___ 17. You work on assignments that other people think are too difficult.

___ 18. You work on long-term projects.

___ 19. You work on short-term projects.

___ 20. You are given more responsibility as you are able to handle it.

___ 21. Your job requires follow-through on all the small details of a project.

___ 22. You get to see your own ideas used in a project.

___ 23. It is your job to pull the various elements of a project together.

___ 24. Your job requires a periodic review or critique by members of the staff.

___ 25. Your job requires a periodic review or critique by your superiors.

___ 26. You are responsible for making major decisions that involve other people.

___ 27. You have no responsibility for decision making.

___ 28. You have a job that allows you to be your own boss.

___ 29. Your job involves being part of a creative team who will depend on your work and your follow-through for their ultimate success with each project.

___ 30. Your job involves a lot of training that you must pick up on your own time.

___ 31. While you are working on a project, you must work directly with your agency's client.

___ 32. To keep up with the work load, you are expected to take work home.

___ 33. Your job often requires you to work evenings and weekends in the office.

___ 34. You are expected to participate in agency presentations to new or prospective clients.

___ 35. Your job requires you to give a periodic review to your co-workers of their work.

___ 36. If you make a mistake on a project, you are expected to correct it on your own time.

___ 37. When you go home from work at night, you can leave your job behind.

___ 38. Your work will be evaluated based on not only your performance but also that of your creative team members.

___ 39. You will be required to put together price quotes for each project you work on.

___ 40. It is your responsibility to make sure your projects stay within the specified budget.

___ 41. You are not directly involved in any of the creative or production work on a project. Instead, it is your job to develop the project's schedule, coordinate each phase of the project, and assign creative and production responsibilities to others.

___ 42. You are responsible for bringing in new business to the agency. Once you do that, you turn over the account to an account coordinator.

___ 43. You bring in new business, and you also work directly with the client and the creative team to implement the project.

___ 44. You are not directly involved in any of the agency's creative or production activities. It is your job to oversee the billing and financial record keeping of the agency.

___ 45. You are in charge of a creative department within the agency. In that capacity you must oversee and supervise your creative team, decide who will work on various aspects of each job, and monitor and tally for final billing all costs involved with each project.

___ 46. Your job with an agency is clerical only, but you have an opportunity to learn and move up to positions of your choosing in the future.

___ 47. Your job is clerical only, and there is no opportunity for advancement. But you will not have the pressure that the creative and management teams face daily. You can enjoy the creative atmosphere around you and still go home with a free mind.

___ 48. You are given many short-term tasks to complete during the work day. These tasks are assigned by your supervisor. You are not responsible for or encouraged to make your own decisions about what you will work on or how your day will be structured.

___ 49. Your position is totally autonomous. You are expected to take charge and anticipate what needs to be done in your department. You structure your own assignments, work whatever number of hours you need to complete a job, and you are free to come and go as you see fit.

___ 50. You must do the majority of your work at home because the office is too distracting to concentrate.

Clarifying your job structure preferences

In the following spaces provided, develop a brief, descriptive listing (as you did in Workshop 2) of all your **A** through **D** statements from Workshop 3.

---

1. My ideal job structure would include the following elements:
   (Briefly list all of your **As**)

   _____

   _____

   _____

   _____

   _____

   _____

   _____

   _____

   _____

   _____

2. I am comfortable with a job structure that includes any of the following: (Briefly list all of your **Bs**)

   _____

   _____

   _____

   _____

   _____

   _____

   _____

   _____

   _____

   _____

3. I am uncomfortable but will accept a job structure that includes any of the following: (Briefly list all of your **C**s)

_____

_____

_____

_____

_____

_____

_____

_____

_____

_____

4. I should avoid a job structure that includes any of the following: (Briefly list all of your **D**s)

_____

_____

_____

_____

_____

_____

_____

_____

_____

Your reasons for preferences help determine guides for compromise

At a glance you can see from Workshop 4 exactly what you would prefer to do and not to do in a job. As with your work environment preferences, it is important to use these as a guide to help you decide which agencies or positions to pursue. And then in the final analysis, when you are making a decision about accepting a certain position, these preferences should be used to evaluate that position. But there will be times when it is wiser to compromise rather than eliminate a position altogether. The thought process you need to go through to decide when and when not to compromise can be mind boggling if you do not understand the deeper, sometimes hidden reasons why some things are more important than others. This process of discovering your true motivations in accepting or rejecting certain elements of a job are rarely black and white.

For example, when it comes down to what is comfortable in a work *environment* for most people, it is usually a matter of what they have gotten used to. While needing a private office is not generally a concern for young people just starting out, others who have worked their way up the ranks to having their own office will be reluctant to give it up. Although there are always exceptions, familiarity is generally the deciding factor in most cases of environmental preference. For this reason people find it easier to compromise, when necessary, on an environmental issue than they do on a question of job structure.

Job *structure* includes the responsibilities you undertake, the pace at which you work, the complexities of your job, and how much you will allow it to infringe on your personal life. These elements have less to do with familiarity. Preferences in these areas tend to touch deep within who we are as individuals. Because of this, it is usually necessary to look closely at your choices when you are called upon to make compromises with your job structure preferences. Compromising is much more difficult here, because your choices and your levels of comfort or discomfort can reflect one of two things: your personal values or a lack of self-confidence in a particular situation.

How personal values and self-confidence affect compromise

If your choice of preference has to do with a personal value, then in most instances you should accept it. People's values do not usually change, unless something traumatic happens in their lives. Values are a part of what makes each of us unique individuals. Along with accepting them, you are better off not compromising your values because sooner or later you will end up blaming yourself for accepting something that went against your personal set of beliefs.

If your choice was motivated by a lack of confidence concerning your ability to handle a required aspect of the job, you will need to think critically about that choice. A lack of self-confidence is a liability to you as an employee. A lack of self-confidence is also a temporary situation which can easily be overcome with a little self-education or professional help, practice, and the willingness to conquer it. Once you recognize that certain choices are based on shaky confidence, not values, then you can decide for yourself if you *can* or *want* to do anything about it. The important thing is to separate your value choices from those that stem from a lack of confidence.

WORKSHOP 5

Deciding when to compromise—values versus confidence

Although you may have exceptions, the decision to compromise on something will only come into question with those statements you labeled as **D**s from either Workshop 1 or 3. Remember your **D**s were those things you hated and would not accept. At the time you labeled them, that was your first reaction to these statements. But now when you look at them again, they may appear differently to you.

Turn back to your descriptive listings in Workshops 2 and 4. Number 4 in each exercise is the listing of all your **D**s. Take each one separately and ask yourself this question: **"If I had to accept this condition or situation, or risk losing a job or job offer, would I do it?"** Perhaps in light of this thought, some of these may not seem quite as objectionable as before. If this applies to any of your listings, put a **check mark** next to it.

These check marks will remind you that these are areas open to compromise. For any that you still feel strongly about, try to imagine how it would feel if you did accept it anyway. Does the thought of having to accept it still make you feel totally uncomfortable or even angry? If so, can you get in touch with why? For example, if you had said that sharing a desk with a part-time employee is something that you would not accept, and the thought of it made you upset inside, then you should ask yourself why. Maybe you would say something like this: "I need my privacy, and obviously, this agency doesn't value me enough to give me my own private space." Or, "I don't want to work for an agency that doesn't have enough room for everyone—that indicates poor planning to me." These reasons are valid, and they probably reflect your values concerning your need for privacy, personal space, or your self-esteem. Trust your feelings. If you can validate or justify any situation that you do not want to accept in either a work environment or a job structure, then you should not compromise in this area.

However, if you look at one of your **D**s, and instead of feeling justified or angry, it makes you feel queasy, uncertain, or downright scared—it may be that this one is coming from a lack of self-confidence. To find out if this is the case, again ask yourself why that particular thing is bothering you. If your answers sound more like excuses, then this may qualify as a confidence issue, not a value judgment.

Examples always help, so here is another one: Suppose you had said that you did not want to accept a job that would require follow-through on small details. When you looked at this a second time, there was that "butterfly" feeling in the pit of your stomach. Okay, lots of folks do not like details. But when you asked yourself why you did not, these were your answers: "I hate fussing over details. They are never that important. I only like the idea stage."

Do these sound like excuses? If so, we can get beneath the surface of your answers and be really honest. In this case, if you were being really honest, you might find yourself saying something like, "Alright, the truth is I always lose track of details. I'm not good at follow-through because I tend to forget things. Look at my desk, it's a mess—I can never find anything. I guess I'm not very well organized." That brings our example down to the bottom line—poor organization. This was the real reason why your reluctance to handle details was causing a feeling of sagging confidence disguised only as a vague sense of discomfort.

If this hypothetical case were real, you would now have to decide the following: "Do I really want to do something about my problem with organization?" If the answer is an overwhelming "no," then leave it alone. Obviously you have decided that this is not open to compromise. It may be that the time just is not right, and you would be forcing yourself to do something that you are not ready for. When the time is right, you will know it. If your answer is "yes," then this issue now becomes a compromisable situation, and you would put a check mark next to this issue.

The only difficult part now might be deciding exactly what remedies to use to correct this new compromisable situation or any other problem that you do want to work on. If you have trouble finding a solution on your own, try talking to a professional career or personal counselor. If you are still in school or a recent graduate, the career placement office will probably have someone in that capacity that can help you. If not, or if you are no longer in school, check the Yellow Pages under career/vocational or therapeutic counseling. The other option could be a good self-help book which may give you the information needed to improve your particular problem areas. A list of recommended books and audio tapes is provided at the end of this book. You can also talk to a trusted teacher or even a friend—someone with more experience in the work world—who can guide you. This can save you a lot of time and frustration when you are casting about for answers and keep coming up empty-handed.

Whatever it is that you finally decide to do, remember that most things about yourself you can change. The key, of course, is wanting to. The more you are able to change those nagging things about yourself that get in the way of your success, the happier you will be as a person. It also follows that the happier you are, the more you will have to offer as a flexible and productive employee. And that is definitely to your benefit as well, because your boss will value your service and be more inclined to contribute to your happiness in the form of raises, promotions, and other added benefits.

Money—how important is it?

Speaking of raises, promotions, and benefits, when it comes to job satisfaction and potential opportunities, just how important is money to you? Most people use money as the deciding factor in accepting a job. They find themselves compromising on work space and job responsibilities while holding firmly to salary and benefit expectations. Is this a wise practice? That all depends on you. If you have a family to feed or a mortgage to pay, then money may indeed be your uncompromisable area. But if you have the luxury of trading up-front financial security or desires for long-term gain, then the trade-offs may be worth it to you.

WORKSHOP 6

Money versus long-term gains

In this workshop, you will examine your feelings about money issues, job satisfaction, and the importance of future opportunities. As with the previous workshops, label each of the "you" statements below with one of the letters **A** through **D**.

[A] I would love it; [B] It would be comfortable; [C] It would be uncomfortable, but I'd accept it; [D] I would hate it, and would not accept it.

____ 1. You are educationally qualified to apply for a job in an agency that you would love to work for. However, you lack the practical experience they prefer. Instead, they offer you an entry level, low paying, trainee position for a specified period of time.

____ 2. The job market is tight, and you are unable to locate an available position in any of the many agencies you have applied to. You can switch to another professional field or you can offer your services to the agency of your choice for no pay until a paying position is available. You then give the agency a time limit of up to three to six months (whichever you can afford) to bring you on in a salaried position or you will leave.

____ 3. You found a terrific position with an agency that is perfect for you in every way. There is only one problem; they want to bring you on as a self-employed freelancer. In this case, you will have to pay your own taxes, health insurance, and there will be no paid holidays.

____ 4. You have been offered a position with the agency you were hoping to go with. Unfortunately, they can only afford to bring you in as a part-time employee until business picks up. They have offered benefits, but cannot guarantee when you will come on board full-time.

____ 5. An agency has offered you a full-time position at a competitive salary and benefits. However, several aspects of your job responsibilities fall into the "unwilling to compromise" category.

___ 6. You have an opportunity to come into one of the best agencies in your area at a salary level that is far below standard. But there is a tremendous potential to learn things you could never pick up at any other agency.

___ 7. You have been offered a position at a reputable agency for a substantial salary and benefits package. The one drawback is that although you are qualified, the job is not in your area of interest. There may be an opportunity to move into another position if one becomes available. But there are no guarantees.

___ 8. You have landed a position at a small agency that will provide you with the opportunity to do just the kind of work you love. However, the job pays less than you wanted. You can survive on that salary, but it will mean making some severe cutbacks for a while.

___ 9. A new but very interesting agency has offered you an opportunity to get in on the ground floor. You will be given a position with a title and responsibilities that are more than you ever hoped for—but at a minimal salary. If the agency grows, you will be made a full partner. The agency owners are willing to put that in writing.

___ 10. An agency is in desperate need of a certain kind of quality work that you in particular have to offer. The agency principals are hoping that your contribution can save the future survival of this agency. In return for your services they are willing to pay you a very high salary and all the benefits you care to negotiate. But if the agency fails in spite of your best efforts, you will be out of a job.

What have you discovered that you did not know already about your attitude toward money and the position that is being offered to you? If your answer is nothing, then you have been in touch with your needs in this area all along. If you have found that you had a difficult time deciding between future opportunities and earning the money you need or want now, then you need to set up some guidelines for yourself.

If money is not the final deciding factor but it is important, then you need to look closely at your personal finances and decide exactly how much you can afford to cut back. Not only in terms of dollars, but also in what you can comfortably give up in your lifestyle. Then whatever you are willing to sacrifice has to be weighed carefully against the opportunity you think can be gained.

The other important thing to look at is whether the opportunity you see is real or has it been fabricated by the agency to lure you into accepting less money. Think about these questions before you jump on the opportunity bandwagon:

- Is this agency really top-notch, and is it worth taking less on the financial end for the experience of working with them?

- Have you talked to other people at this agency to see if what is offered prior to accepting a position is what is truly expected once you are hired?

  Even if the agency owners have agreed to put it in writing that you will be made a full partner, be sure the terms and conditions are spelled out before you accept the job. For example:

TRAITS OF SUCCESSFUL FREELANCERS

In my experience as a former freelancer and an agency owner who has worked with dozens of freelancers, those who survived and thrived possessed certain common characteristics. These characteristics make these individuals noticeably different from the typical employee.

Successful freelancers tend to be:

- more focused on what their client wants from a project than how much they will make on the project
- willing to spend more time to produce a quality piece of work than they will be able to charge for
- self-directed, requiring little or no supervision to begin work
- outgoing and friendly
- unruffled when it comes to picking up the phone or walking in to an agency to solicit work
- inately aware of how to diffuse a potentially hostile person when things begin to go wrong
- gently persistent
- less motivated by their ego and more motivated by their love for the work they do
- amazed that they get paid for doing the work they love
- excellent at attending to every possible detail
- more than willing to admit when they have made a mistake
- responsible for becoming better and better at what they do
- unwilling to settle for mediocre ideas, craftsmanship, and results
- very attentive to follow through during a project—they always do what they promised they would do
- comfortable taking full responsibility for every aspect of a project
- meticulous about checking to be sure that other people involved in the production of a project are aware of deadlines, expectations, and responsibilities
- unwilling to leave things to chance
- clear about what they do well, what they love to do, and what areas they are weakest in
- careful about getting into something over their heads, yet open to new challenges as long as the client won't suffer in the learning
- excited about their own work, not from ego but from pure enthusiasm
- problem solvers by nature
- good with finances, staying within their client's budget and paying their own bills on time
- genuinely grateful for each client.

- What criteria do the owners use to determine when the agency has grown enough to bring you into the partnership?

- Is there a time limit on their offer?

- How do you know that you will even want to be in a partnership with these people if you do not know them?

Remember that all partners are responsible for the bills generated by the business if one or more of the partners disappears or is unable to meet financial obligations. Before you make any final decisions that involve a potential opportunity—financial or experiential—ask around for the opinions and viewpoints of trusted friends and business associates. Others may be able to shed some light into dark corners that you could not see or they may know something or someone you did not. If all checks out and you still feel that this is a good deal, then go ahead.

To check out the stability and business reputation of any agency, begin first with local vendors (printers, typesetters, photographers, freelancers) and art supply stores and media companies (radio, television, and newspapers) that might do business with that agency. Several phone calls to the owners or sales representatives of companies and businesses that have worked with the agency in question should give you more than enough information about whether the agency pays its bills on time, is generally considered reputable in the business community, and has congenial employees. You can also call the Better Business Bureau in your area to see if any complaints have ever been filed against the agency. If you want the real scoop on an agency's financial stability, you can talk to any credit bureau listed in your local phone book. However, there may be a fee for a credit report. Finally, you can call your local office of Dun & Bradstreet to see if the agency is listed and, if so, what their business is rated. If an agency is a member of the American Association of Advertising Agencies (AAAA) you can check with them on the agency's status. Do keep in mind that there are many perfectly reputable agencies that never join the Better Business Bureau, AAAA, or Dun & Bradstreet, so don't be discouraged if you come up empty-handed with any of these organizations.

The final lap of your job search

When you have completed all eight steps outlined in this book and you are close to making a decision on which of hopefully several positions you will accept, it is important that you remember what you have learned from these exercises—about yourself, your work preferences, and financial needs. You should restrict your choices to only those jobs that meet your personal needs and requirements. This will be a difficult thing to do when the time comes, since most people are so eager and anxious to get a job that they often sacrifice or forget what is really necessary to keep them functioning at their best.

Before I bring this chapter to a close, I do want to make it clear that I am not advocating the prima donna attitude of "I will only do what I want to do in a job." That outlook will not get anyone very far. Instead, these exercises were intended to put you in touch with what is right for you in a job. I have seen far too many employees and prospective employees who have little, if any, idea about what they need to do their jobs well. I am still amazed at the number of talented and capable people who finally leave the advertising profession altogether, following one shattering experience after another, simply because they kept accepting positions that were not suited to their personalities or their abilities.

Choose an area of specialization

Find a niche

A *niche* is described by *Webster's New World Dictionary* as an especially suitable place or position. In Step One you examined the importance of determining the type of work environment, job functions, and responsibilities that were best suited to your personality. Having established your personal criteria, you have already created one kind of niche for yourself—we will call that a "work mode" niche. In addition to that, you will need to find another niche—an area of specialization that relates to advertising. This niche should be geared to your particular skills, talents, personality type, and a high score on an interest/love rating scale.

"But why," you may ask, "do I need an area of specialization when I am just beginning to get into advertising?" Having an area of specialization will enable you to concentrate your full attention and focus in one direction once you do get into advertising. **Full concentration in just one area at a time is the only pathway to mastery.** And while you may not need to be a master in a specialized area to get a job in advertising, the intent to work toward mastering an area of specialization will be respected by any potential employer. Obviously the person who is flexible and willing to take on any job or challenge will also be attractive to an employer. But if that flexibility and willingness is balanced with the motivation and follow-through to be the best designer, copywriter, researcher, or whatever it is that you are capable of being, you will be a rare and highly revered employee long after the initial glow of your flexibility has worn thin on your boss's list of valuable qualities. Getting a job involves more than the short-term enthusiasm of the eager fledgling. It means being able to demonstrate to an interested employer that you understand what successful employees are made of: the desire and dedication to be outstanding.

SPECIALIZED AREAS FOR FREELANCERS

While agencies will hire freelancers for just about any aspect of design or production that may need to be done when their own staff is over-burdened, there are certain things that agencies turn to freelancers for on a regular basis. If your skills and interests are in line with any of these areas, you will most likely find yourself with a steady stream of freelance work.

- Illustration—especially specialized areas such as fashion, technical, or medical, that have a unique style
- Typesetting
- Computer graphics
- Mechanical preparation—especially for large jobs like annual reports and catalogs that can tie up agency staffers
- Photography
- Videography
- Design work—if the designer has a desirable, outstanding style
- Production management—smaller agencies will often hire a freelancer to take a project from start to finish because they don't have the in-house staff to do it
- Copywriting—even agencies with a copy department frequently want fresh ideas or they use freelancers when their own staff is backed up with work
- Typography—designers who specialize in designing with type are frequently sought out by agencies for identity packages and logo development
- Media scheduling and buying—many small agencies are turning to media specialists to recommend and purchase their media rather than keeping a person on staff to do so
- Bookkeeping/accounting—agencies of all sizes are more inclined to hire independent bookkeepers and accountants as needed

To be successful in advertising or any profession, for that matter, you must be outstanding. That means you must rise above the mass level of mediocrity. Most people think that the ability to be outstanding is something that only a few people are born with—a talent or a gift. A good many of these same people are convinced that they are not one of the lucky few. Thus, they are content to settle for "good enough," and therein lies the origin of mediocrity. When members of the mediocre masses are presented with the notion that to become outstanding in your profession is not really a matter of talent, nor is it a gift, but rather it is a matter of self-discipline and concentrated hard work, they say: "Maybe so, but they don't pay me enough around here to work that hard!" The truth is no one will ever pay you to *become* outstanding. They will only pay you enough when you *are* outstanding. So becoming outstanding is entirely your own responsibility.

Discipline and concentrated hard work are the keys to becoming outstanding. Discipline means consistent efforts to do one thing over and over, striving to get a little better each time—even when you do not feel like doing it. Concentration is the ability to be single-minded in your attentions toward an activity. With discipline and concentration you cannot help but get better at something. Combine that with focus in an area of specialization and you have the proven formula for becoming outstanding.

So if you are one of those people who does not have a specialization niche and you are just floating along saying, "I want to work in advertising and I'm willing to do just about anything," you will need to revise your thinking. Otherwise, you may get exactly what you want—a job in advertising doing anything and everything that no one else wants to do. And as time goes by, you will still be answering the phone, running errands, and doing odd jobs around the office while other people will be promoted from assistant art director to senior art director, junior copywriter to copy chief, and so on.

Maybe you already think you know the area of specialization or niche you want to work in. Maybe it is because you have a degree in that area or years of experience and you are good at it. But before you close the book (no pun intended) on other possibilities, let us see if what you have chosen matches your personality type, and how it rates when you come to do the Area of Specialization Evaluation workshop at the end of Step Three.

WORKSHOP 7

What is your personality type?

Sometimes you have to look beyond training and experience to find the area of specialization that fits with your personality type. If you decide to specialize in a particular area that is incompatible with your personality type, in time you will find yourself growing discontent and frustrated with your choice. In advertising, the division of people into "types" falls into three specific categories: visuals, verbals, and all business types. Knowing your specific type or combination of types will help you decide what areas of specialization or what niches are just right for you.

Suppose you have always thought that you wanted to be a graphic designer but, until now, never knew that you were not a visual type. After reading this chapter, you have decided that your personality is much more in line with the verbal types. As you review the many jobs you could do in advertising, you begin to realize that you have ignored for years that you love to write. Because your artistic/design skills were recognized and rewarded early in your life by parents, teachers, and friends, you just naturally thought you would study design. And somewhere along the line, you let your interest in writing slip away. Now you understand that by resurrecting your love for writing and using it in advertising you would be much happier than exclusively limiting yourself to design work. In fact, you would be a greater asset to an agency as a copywriter/designer—which is a rare combination.

Visual types

Visuals are those people who tend to think in terms of visual images. If you say to them, "this is such garbage," they will immediately get a picture in their minds of slop, goop, and junk spilling out from a green plastic garbage can. These are the same people who speak in phrases like: "I *see* what you mean." Or, "I *see* how that could happen." When they make jokes, these usually involve visual puns.

Visuals are often drawn toward artistic endeavors and interests. Whether it is a form of painting, drawing, sculpture, or dance, they usually become involved in some capacity with the visual arts at an early age. Those who do not possess a natural talent for performance in one of these artistic areas may find a more passive outlet for their interests such as art critic or avid collector of the arts. Those with the ability tend to want to become artists of some sort. Unfortunately, many visuals are told early on by parents, teachers, and the like that it is tough to make a living as an artist. Those who believe this usually abandon their lofty ambitions and go into advertising. The dreamer who wants to be a painter becomes an illustrator or designer, the sculptor becomes a model maker or package designer, and the printmaker turns to computer graphics, and so it goes. I say this with a note of cynicism because it is tough to make a living as an artist, but it is equally tough to make a living in advertising, too. Both pursuits require that you be outstanding in order to make a "good living." So if you have chosen advertising in lieu of the fine arts, be sure it is because you love it, not because you think it will be easier.

The visuals who do go into advertising usually lean toward one of the following areas of specialization: art direction, graphic design, illustration, photography, videography, typesetting or typography.

Art direction

An art director's primary job responsibility is to work closely with a copywriter and creative director to develop the main idea concepts for an advertising campaign or an individual project. Once a specific concept has been determined, the art director and copywriter work together to unite the words and graphic images. From this point, the art director may also be responsible for producing rough thumbnail layouts or may opt to turn this phase of the project over to a graphic designer. The art director then supervises the graphic designer's progress from rough layout to presentation format through final completed piece.

Graphic design

Graphic design is the spatial arrangement of various elements (form, line, texture, color, and type) on a two-dimensional surface. Structural design involves the manipulation of the same elements, but on a three-dimensional surface. Package designers, set designers, and model makers are concerned with structure although their job function is often referred to as a form of graphic design.

In an advertising agency, graphic designers work on projects that range from the design of newspaper and magazine ads, brochures, newsletters, catalogs, and annual reports to logos, business cards, stationery, vehicle and building signage, posters, charts, and graphs. They can also become involved in package design, modelmaking, and point of purchase and store displays. While someone may choose to become a graphic designer, the exact area of specialization will vary because of personal preference and ability, exposure to one area more than another, or on-the-job demand.

Illustration

If you want to be an illustrator, you should already know that you have the talent and skill to draw exceptionally well. Providing that skill and talent are a given, then you will need a thorough grounding in design principles and extensive experience with a variety of drawing mediums. Beyond that, every illustrator hopes for two things: to develop a unique and recognizable style, and the creative ability to approach each assignment with a fresh and unusual point of view. Illustrators who simply draw well or render objects accurately will not find a ready market for their work. Photography is a constant competitor when it comes to depicting reality. Illustration, to be a valuable substitute, must go beyond what a photograph is capable of portraying—it must radiate an aura of the illustrator's inner vision in a way that a camera cannot begin to capture.

Photography

Photographers who work in advertising produce photographs that either depict an image of a client's product, service, or the end user the client is trying to reach. The kind of photograph (i.e., black and white, color, subject matter, and viewer appeal) that will be used in an ad is most often determined by the art director. The photographer may be asked to contribute opinions and ideas about the photographic concept, but final judgment is generally reserved for the art director. However, the photographer's expertise is counted on when it comes to the technical elements of the finished photograph, the lighting, and the atmospheric quality the photographer is able to achieve.

Videography

Video is rapidly becoming an important adjunct to agency business. At one time, television commercials were exclusively shot on 16mm or 35mm film, edited, and then transferred to videotape to enable the stations to air them. But now with the tremendous improvements in the reproduction quality of videotape, many commercials are exclusively produced in video format. Since video is considerably less expensive than film, this has enabled agencies to offer quality television commercial production to clients whose budget restrictions had previously prevented them from considering this medium.

Film production is still the first choice of agencies whose clients can afford to use it. The clarity and trueness in color still cannot be matched with video. Although the average television viewer usually cannot tell the difference when they watch a local car dealership spot produced on video followed by a filmed commercial for a national company like Coke, Pepsi, or IBM, it is glaringly apparent to the trained eye. But video is definitely here to stay, and the future promises that the quality improvement in video production will continue at a rapid pace.

Typesetting

Typesetters are the backbone of the advertising industry. These are the people who set the type used in print ads, brochures, catalogs, annual reports, logos, signage—anything and everything that contains printed words.

Typesetting methods have become highly sophisticated in the past twenty years. This is due to rapid advancements in computerized digital typesetting equipment and expansion in the design of fonts and special display type. In addition, typesetting equipment is now able to manipulate type to create dramatic effects such as distortion, slanting, and setting type on curves, circles, and angles. This has allowed the typesetter and graphic designer far greater latitude in their creative expression.

Typography

The study of typography includes the history of type, how to design type styles, and the use of type as an integral part of graphic design. Professional typographers often specialize in the design of typefaces, or some become graphic designers who concentrate on the use of type as the main design element in their work.

Verbal types

Verbal types love words—written words, spoken words—any words at all. They think in words—not images—unlike their visual counterparts. Some say verbally-inclined people are dominated by the left side of the brain where symbolism, logic, and sequential thinking takes place. I do not know for sure about that, but I do know that verbal types seem to possess more than their share of logic, and they are definitely sequential thinkers (one thought leads to the next, which leads to the next, and so on).

Because of their fascination with words, as small children these verbal types were the ones who could not wait to get their first library card. When they did, these young verbals carried home armloads of books and would often hide out in the quietest part of the house, happily reading the day away. Meanwhile, their little visual friends were out playing ball, climbing trees, or drawing all over the sidewalk. Verbals usually emerge as adults who have a strong interest in literature—whether that involves writing, reading, or critiquing it. They may be drawn as well to foreign languages or the study of any discipline that requires a great deal of reading or writing. With their highly developed sense of logic and sequential thinking, verbals may also lean towards mathematics and science. But remember that few people are all verbal or all visual in orientation and thought process. Most are a bit of both with a strong inclination one way or the other.

Like visuals, verbals are also often drawn toward the arts. Many yearn to become playwrights, novelists, or poets. Also like their visual siblings, they have been told that writers cannot earn a decent living. So verbals turn to advertising, public relations, publishing, journalism, teaching, and all those other equally respectable word-oriented professions. Those that do choose advertising usually find themselves in one of two job specialities: copywriting or research.

Copywriters

Copywriters work with art directors and creative directors to produce the various elements of an ad campaign. Copywriters provide the words; art directors, the images; and creative directors, the inspiration or the spark.

Copywriting takes a special talent—the ability to paint a picture in the reader's mind with words. That picture must then be so appealing that it makes the reader want what is in it. This applies not only to written words but also the words that are heard in a radio or television commercial.

Research

Contrary to popular notions about advertising, creative ideas and positioning strategies are not simply pulled from thin air. Advertising professionals base every concept, slogan, television and radio commercial, print ad, billboard—virtually every message-carrying vehicle used—on thorough market research, product history, competitor's activities, and the demographics of the audience to be reached. When a campaign is over, follow-up research is usually done on the effect the campaign had on its audience.

Researchers are the scouts and detectives of the advertising industry. They seek out all of the relevant information necessary to build a campaign, then compile and present it to the agency's creative people and the account service team. Verbals who are more comfortable reading than writing are often drawn toward the research end of agency work.

All business types

The *all business types* come from every imaginable educational background. They can be either verbal or visual in orientation, although their inclination for pragmatism and logic definitely tilts them toward the verbal side of the scale. The all business types do share one common denominator: they understand that the all important, delicate balance between client and agency must be maintained at all costs. They know that this important balance directly translates to bottom-line profits and agency growth.

The all business types know without a doubt that regardless of their personal contributions to agency work in the form of creative output, client service, or even their particular status in the agency that without the agency *they* cease to exist in a business sense. Thus, the all business types are company-centered men and women. Because these people understand how business works, they are most often drawn to positions in which they either deal directly with clients or into areas of specialization that enable them to translate their innate sense of business acumen into agency activities directly related to marketing, finance, and negotiation.

The all business types include: account executives, account supervisors, marketing directors, media planners and buyers, and business managers.

Account executives

Account executives "bring home the bacon" in an advertising agency. The art, copy, and production people "fry it up in the pan," which the account executives then "serve" to the clients and pray they will love it. If rejected it is the account executive who takes the heat. And here, in this simplistic analogy, is the ever-present rub between an agency's creative team and the all business types.

While the creatives are working their little hearts out to produce something that will make peoples' eyes pop, the account executives are worried about their client's budget, the interpersonal dynamics between themselves and the client, and, ultimately, the client's satisfaction. Personally, I think account work is one of the most difficult parts of advertising because you are always forced to walk a tightrope between what you know is the best thing for the client and what clients think they want.

Media planners and buyers

Media planners work together with the marketing and creative people to tailor each campaign to the targeted audience group. Once the appropriate creative strategy has been established, the media specialists will recommend which media to use for the campaign and what percentage of the client's budget to dedicate to each selection.

Depending on the agency, media planners can also be media buyers. This is generally the case with smaller agencies. The larger agencies, however, do have enough volume to keep a media planner so busy that a media buyer is essential to complete the agency's media cycle.

Buyers take the media schedule developed by the planners and contact each of the selected radio and television stations, newspapers, magazines, billboard companies, and any other media vendors the planners have recommended. Sometimes that can even include sky writers or balloon companies. Working with each of the media's own representatives, buyers communicate exactly what the final schedule breaks down to, in terms of money to be spent versus the number of advertisements that can be purchased for that amount. The most important skill a media buyer must possess is the ability to negotiate the best possible price for each media buy.

Business managers

Business managers oversee agency finances. That includes monitoring all project cost records, preparing client bills, and supervising bookkeepers and secretaries to make sure incoming bills are properly recorded and paid on time. They also make recommendations to management on agency spending and financial planning, and work with the agency's accountant to prepare year-end financial statements.

Business managers are the heartbeat of an advertising agency because without their careful attention to financial details the agency would be out of business in no time.

It takes all kinds

There are three more niches that require such a vast cross section of skills that it is nearly impossible to say whether the people who are drawn to these areas are of one particular type or another. More specifically, the following positions seem to be inundated with people who possess a well-rounded combination of visual, verbal, and all business attributes. In other words, it takes all kinds to fill the openings in these agency niches: secretary, traffic coordinator, production coordinator, account coordinator, and creative director.

Secretary

Secretaries in ad agencies are some of the most important team members. They become the support for any creative, management, or sales team. Aside from the typical office management functions that secretaries perform in an ad agency, secretaries are greatly valued if they are capable of editing ad copy, proposals, and client letters, along with troubleshooting budgets, billing, financial reports, and media schedules. In addition, secretaries are frequently asked to participate in creative brainstorm sessions and client meetings. Their opinions and insights to campaign concepts and creative strategies are welcomed by art directors and copywriters who can get too close to the creative process.

Traffic coordinator

Imagine an advertising agency as a giant intersection with roads coming in from every possible direction. Each road represents a new project coming in to the agency. In the middle of the intersection, at a very large desk, sits the traffic coordinator. The traffic coordinator quite literally gives an account executive a red or green signal for each new project they bring into the agency, because the traffic coordinator is the person in charge of scheduling and controlling the flow of agency work.

Production coordinator

This is the partner position to the traffic coordinator. The two work closely together—constantly feeding each other information back and forth. The traffic coordinator schedules a job only after an update from the production coordinator as to exactly where everything stands with each ongoing project in the production department.

The production coordinator is not always the most popular person in an agency. That is because they are vigilant watchdogs who have to follow the progress of each project as it passes through agency production and hound everyone involved to be sure they stay on schedule. Bodily injury is frequently threatened when someone lags behind a deadline. Sometimes they have to be merciless to keep production moving smoothly.

Account coordinator

Account coordinators have been known to save the necks of many an account executive. As account executives' right arms, account coordinators keep track of all of the activity generated by each account they are assigned to. When some detail is about to fall through the cracks, it is often the account coordinator who catches the problem after it has slipped right by everyone else.

Account coordinators are in constant contact with the traffic and production coordinators to update them on the status of various projects or when a particular account is about to become active. No account is constantly active; they all have their seasons. And all agency people thank their lucky stars for that. Imagine if every account an agency had was active all the time. An agency would have to be ten times its size just to handle that much work.

Account supervisor

Following a successful track record as an account executive, the next step up is usually to that of account supervisor. I say *usually* because there are those individuals who are not interested in the management arena of agency business. They like working directly with the clients and prefer to avoid supervisory responsibilities.

Account supervisors are exactly that—supervisors who monitor a specified number of accounts and the account executives who service them. They are also ultimately responsible for the coordination and final results generated by each account executive assigned to those accounts.

Marketing director

Marketing directors are mostly found in the larger to middle-sized agencies. They work closely with the research department to stay current on new market trends, socio-economic conditions, and marketplace competition. When the research team feeds the marketing directors new information factors, these people analyze the data and make recommendations to both the client and the creative people in the agency on the best strategy to use when approaching an advertising campaign.

When a smaller agency hires a person with a background in marketing, it generally brings that person in as an account executive since small agencies cannot afford the luxury of a full-time market specialist.

Creative director

Creative directors work with copywriters and art directors to develop the creative concepts that will be used in specific campaigns and projects. It is the creative director's responsibility to encourage the creative team to explore all avenues of possibility as they work to develop a useable creative approach to a project. The creative director is the team's inspiration, the spark that ignites their flame. Once the team is ignited, the creative director then fans that flame to keep it burning brightly throughout the entire length of the project.

Creative directors also must evaluate all the ideas that are proposed by the creative team and then make the final decisions as to which ones are the best.

They then pass their recommendations on to the account executive in charge of that project. In addition, creative directors monitor the progress of each project as it goes through production, to be certain that it is in line with the initial concept and serves the needs of the client.

When you reach the rank of creative director, you and everyone around you will know that you are a seasoned professional. You have most likely earned your stripes in either the art or copy department as an outstanding performer. You have proven beyond a doubt that you can be consistently counted upon to come up with exciting concepts. You also have proven that you have the ability to inspire and lead a team of other creative people to perform in a superior manner.

Take the next step

At this point, you may feel confident that you have selected an area of specialization, a niche that feels right to you. That is great, but before you dash off and revise the *Career Objectives* section of your resume to reflect your chosen specialty, you still need a bit more information. You may think that being an art director or an account executive sounds like your cup of tea, but first you need to know if you have the right combination of personality traits, training, skills, and interest.

Those of you who are still uncertain about the direction you want to pursue in advertising may just need more information. Or perhaps you have not read enough, yet, that relates to you. Even though nothing is clicking for you right now, it will—that is, if you are meant to be in advertising. There will be some people who, after reading everything about all the different types of jobs, still will not have a strong personal reaction to any of them. If you find that happens to you, then advertising may not be in your deck of cards. You may have been looking at this profession for the wrong reasons. Maybe you have been drawn to it because it looks like fun or people have told you that advertising is where the action or money is. Or maybe you just always assumed that you would go into advertising because you thought it was interesting enough to get a degree in it. If any of this rings true for you, you may need to take a few steps backward and try to understand what led you to advertising in the first place. If you can get back to this root, you may be able to discover what other options you can explore that will put to use your own special blend of talents, skills, and interests.

Step Three will tell you more about the specific job responsibilities in each niche or area of specialization. It will also present the educational or experiential qualifications you should have to pursue these areas and describe something about the kind of person who functions well in each of these positions. Then at the end of the chapter, you can do the Area of Specialization Evaluation workshop. This will help you sort through and evaluate all the reactions you have had while reading Step Two and Step Three. Upon completing the workshop you should know what areas of specialization are right for you and why.

Focus in on the niche

Fit the niche

Selecting a niche that seems custom-made for you is not just a matter of thinking that this area sounds great or that it is right for you because of your education and training. Instead, if the niche is right for you, it has to fit who you are, hold your interest, and keep you feeling passionate about the work you have chosen to do.

To help you with the decision-making process of exploring your options and evaluating them we will take an even closer look at each of the specialized areas or niches presented in Step Two and examine:

- The nature of the job
- The kind of individual who performs well in this particular niche
- The talent, education, and training each niche demands in the advertising marketplace.

WORKSHOP 8

Do you fit the niche?

In workshop 7 you were asked to **check off** those positions that you found interesting or attractive. You were also instructed to **highlight** or **underline** any aspects of those jobs you related to. I would like you to do the same in this chapter with any of the qualifications, job descriptions, or personality traits that seem to apply to you. You will need to refer back to this personal inventory in the Area of Specialization Evaluation exercise at the end of Step Three.

Art direction

Art directors often begin their careers as paste-up artists and then become graphic designers. From there, with increased experience, they will take on more management and supervisory responsibilities. Depending on the agency's needs, a graphic designer will move up in the agency echelon to the positions of junior and senior art director. The time this upward movement may take depends entirely on the individual's capabilities, the agency's size, and its internal structure. In general, promotions come sooner in smaller agencies.

Almost without exception, art directors will need at least two years of college preparation as design, graphics, or fine arts majors. Many art directors, however, do have either four year or even graduate degrees.

Some agencies involve the art directors, copywriters, and creative directors in the initial client meetings to hear first hand what the client wants. Later they are included in the formal presentation meeting to assist the account executive in explaining to the client why a particular creative strategy was chosen and how the words and graphic images reflect that strategy. Once the client has approved the final concept for a campaign project, the art director oversees the production of all mechanicals for print materials as well as other support mediums such as television commercials, training tapes, or slide presentations. The art director's main objective is to be sure that all visual elements of the campaign have a consistent image.

In many agencies, especially the smaller ones, art directors are also in charge of scheduling and pricing out the projects that go through their department. For example, if an agency is producing an annual report for a client, once the concept has been developed and a budget established (usually by the client), the art director then determines the printing specifications (finished size, paper stock, number of pages, colors, photos and/or illustrations to be used) and passes this information on to several printing companies for price quotes. At the same time, quotes are gathered from photographers, illustrators, typesetters, and any other outside sources whose services may be needed to complete the project. Once the quotes are in and compared, the art director will then decide which companies will be selected to handle the final execution of the various jobs.

It is important to note that the art director's decision is not always based on the least expensive quote. It is based on a fair market price plus the company's ability to complete the job on time, stay within the quote, and do the best quality work. This delicate combination of requirements makes the final selection a difficult decision, especially if the company or freelancer is unfamiliar. That is why a good reputation is so essential in business. When prices and time frames are equal, reputation is the next deciding factor. And quite often a good reputation will justify higher prices.

When the outside sources have been selected and final prices established, the art director meets with the copy department, layout and mechanical artists, as well as outside source people to determine a workable production schedule. As the project evolves, the art director is ultimately responsible for monitoring costs on aspects of the project generated in the art department such as type, printing, photography, mechanicals, and illustrations. The copy department oversees copywriting, research, and interview costs.

Graphic design

Although some people have been known to pick it up on their own, most graphic designers have formal training. That is because designing graphics is not based merely on personal taste or the haphazard placement of lines and shapes on a two-dimensional surface, as clients are often inclined to think; it is based on solid design theory, patterns of eye movement, and the psychological effects of color, pattern, and texture. The study and application of these methods date back to the early Greeks and Romans. I am always sardonically amused when a client says of an ad or brochure layout, "Just make it pretty." Pretty has nothing to do with it. Pretty is a personal opinion that varies with each individual. Good, sound design involves a myriad of complex elements that are all interdependent. If you change one element (which clients love to do) that changes the relationship of everything else in that space. That means the entire space will have to be redesigned to accommodate any changes.

Computer graphics   A whole new field in graphic design is opening up with the advanced technology of computer graphics. Most art and design schools and an increasing number of college and university design programs now offer a wide variety of courses in computer graphics. While the most popular computer graphics course is still desktop publishing, there are many other courses that involve the use of computers in illustration, producing camera-ready art, logo design, video graphics, animation, and three-dimensional design. Desktop publishing is a generic term for a number of programs available that are capable of producing page layouts and typesetting for newsletters, brochures, and other types of publications. Many agencies presently use computers in some capacity for design and typesetting, and this trend will continue to grow rapidly. The more you know about the application of computers to the field of graphic design, the more attractive you will be to an agency.

Graphic design breaks down into two distinct job activities.

Layout design   When a general concept for a project (print ad, logo, billboard, brochure, etc.) has been decided upon by the client, account executive, and agency creative people (art director, copywriter, creative director, etc.), a graphic designer is then asked to develop a series of rough sketches or layouts to illustrate a number of different ways this concept could be visually developed. Using tracing paper, the designer begins to explore a variety of visual options in the form of tiny drawings called thumbnails (because of their small size, usually no larger than one or two inches). In these initial layout sketches, all of the elements that must go into the finished project are loosely laid down in pencil or colored markers.

These sketches will indicate where the type could be placed in relation to the photos or illustrations and then in conjunction with any copy that might be used.

A designer will often do as many as fifty different thumbnail variations before deciding which layout works the best. This may seem like a lot of work, but that is where true creativity begins to unfold. If you remember, my definition of creativity earlier in the book stated that creativity is simply the act of finding as many different solutions as possible to any given problem. That means you cannot settle for three solutions or even ten when there might be more if you keep working at it. Once the greatest number of solutions have been explored, then finding the best solution—the most creative solution—will be evident because you will have it right there in front of you. You will not have to guess or wonder if the idea you have selected to work with is the best possible solution; you will be able to see that by comparison all those other thumbnail designs clearly do not work as well.

When a variety of thumbnails have been completed, the designer will usually select several of the best for translation into larger presentation layouts. These layouts will have a more finished, polished look because they will be used to present the best of the ideas to the client. Even though the designer may think that one design in particular outranks the others, it is always wise to present three or four other possibilities, because psychologically, clients like to feel that they have a choice. In addition, the designer has already had the experience of seeing which of the many layouts worked the best. By selecting only one to show to a client, the client has no way of understanding the designer's thought process and why this one design was apparently the best solution. Working with clients is an ongoing process of gentle education—helping them to see the complex issues that must be considered before making a final decision that will determine what their project will look like and if it will achieve the desired results.

When the client has selected a preferred layout, the designer will then prepare a comprehensive layout. This layout, often called a "comp," looks as close to the real thing as possible. Executed in actual size, either by hand or computer generated, it displays the type style that will be used, the point size of the type, how the photos or illustrations will interrelate with the type and other graphic elements, and any changes the client may have requested in the rough thumbnail sketch stage. This final layout will usually go through one more round of client approvals before being sent on to typesetting.

While the type is being ordered, the photos or illustrations can be prepared if necessary and all other details of the project, such as printing schedules, prices, production schedules, etc., can be coordinated and reviewed one last time. When all of the finished elements of the project have been completed (type, photos, illustrations), the designer will then be ready to begin the mechanical.

Most graphic designers will be involved in all phases of design production, from conception through finished mechanical. However, some graphic designers may prefer to specialize exclusively in layout art in which they are responsible for only the concept development and comprehensive stages of a graphics project. The final mechanical preparation is then left to a mechanical artist, also called a board artist or paste-up artist.

Mechanical preparation   Mechanical preparation is translation of a design, such as an ad, a brochure, or a poster into a piece of flat art that can be used to make a print. This is accomplished by pasting the finished elements of the design—type, position stats to indicate where photographs and/or illustrations will be placed, ruby overlays for color separations, product or company logos, and any other pertinent materials that will appear in the finished piece—onto a flat surface such as smooth, white mat board or blue-lined tara board. This completed board or paste-up is called a mechanical. Mechanicals are often referred to as camera-ready art because the printer will produce a photographic negative directly from the mechanical. The negative is then used to create a metal plate from which the final piece will be printed.

Preparing mechanicals is a job that requires more training and experience than actual artistic talent. A neophyte entering an agency with little practical experience will often start out doing very basic paste-ups on mechanicals while working under the wing of a more experienced board artist. This is an excellent way to begin. No matter how much background one has had in classroom design theory, schools are not able to prepare a student with the variety of experiences necessary to develop the skills needed to be a fast and accurate mechanical artist. And being fast and accurate is the main requirement any agency will expect from a full-fledged mechanical artist. From here a designer can move up into layout design and eventually art direction and creative direction.

Those people who choose to spend their entire careers in advertising as mechanical specialists have to be a certain type of individual. While specializing in mechanical prep can certainly be very rewarding work, the people who do it, and do it well, must be sticklers for minute details. They must also have a knack for knowing when something is visually correct—that is, when lines of type are straight and parallel, the edges of a shape are square, or the measurement and placement of things appear proportionally accurate. They have to have a good eye for judging the accuracy of their mechanicals, because deadlines are constantly hanging over their heads and there is not always time to measure and check everything. In addition, mechanical artists must be fastidiously neat, as mechanicals cannot have smudges, nicks, or anything out of place. They must also be able to balance the ability to review every element of the mechanical to be sure nothing has been left out, yet sure enough of their own methodical execution process that they do not over-review unnecessarily.

Illustration

Unless you are employed by a fairly large ad agency, it will be difficult to work in an agency as a full-time illustrator. Illustrations are not used on a regular basis in most advertising projects. The reason is that marketing surveys prove that the public responds more readily to photographs than they do to illustrations. A photograph is a mirror of reality, an illustration is the artist's interpretation of it. Reality sells; interpretations do not.

Illustrations do have a place in advertising when it comes to the kind of representations a camera cannot achieve. For example, when the tone of an advertisement calls for an exaggeration or manipulation of forms or the effect that can be created by a montage of multiple images, an illustration can easily achieve these results. Illustrations also work well for those circumstances when an object needs to be represented in a diagrammatic three-dimensional view that can expose both the interior and exterior surfaces at once. Illustrations are also used for certain types of products that do not reproduce well photographically—especially in newspapers where the finer tonalities tend to drop out. This applies particularly to furniture, cameras, appliances, automobiles, and other items with reflective or textured surfaces.

Illustrators who do want to work full-time for an advertising agency will also need to be competent graphic designers and paste-up artists. This combination will make them very attractive to a potential employer.

However, if your heart and soul is only in illustration, then you may have much better luck as a freelancer. Freelancers can work for many different agencies and companies that use illustrators. In this way you can pick and choose the assignments that will give you an opportunity to fully develop a unique style and creative approach. If you are eventually able to achieve that individualized quality in your work and your work is good, chances are favorable that you will make a decent living as an illustrator. Of course, to be a freelancer you will also have to be a self-starter, develop a strong sense of personal discipline, and have sound business skills. You will be running your own business, and you will be totally responsible for its financial success as well as its financial liabilities.

Since this book is about finding a job in an advertising agency, I will not spend a lot of time presenting the various opportunities available for illustrators outside of advertising. But if you would like to explore alternative avenues of employment, illustrators are in greater demand in areas such as publishing, printing, fashion, architecture, film animation, and certain industries where products must be rendered on a regular basis, such as the manufacturing and jewelry industries. Illustrators are also an essential part of companies that require specialized technical drawing skills, such as scientific and medical illustration, engineering and conceptual design.

Creative director

A creative director in an advertising agency is like an orchestra's conductor. The creative director leads and inspires the copywriters, art directors, and graphic designers to rise to a peak of creative excitement and inspiration. When a new project comes in, the creative director meets with the account executive and sometimes even the client to determine the project's parameters. Following recommendations from research and marketing, the creative director meets with the art and copy people to brainstorm ideas. These creative jam sessions are the stuff that TV sitcoms and movies are made of: The wild and crazy copywriters jump up from their chairs with an incredibly brilliant campaign slogan, followed by an ever-so-clever "doowop" jingle. Suddenly the art director is moved to scribble a masterpiece design on an oversized drawing pad, as the creative director continues to stir the group to a fevered crescendo.

Some creative directors insist on total control over all the final elements in the concept development of a campaign or project. That can be a very dangerous position to take. The rest of the creative staff that must work with this type of director usually end up feeling like minions. The best kind of creative director is an enthusiastic and compassionate leader who has the ability to make everyone in the creative group feel their input is valued—even when it cannot be used.

Creative directors come from a variety of advertising backgrounds. Some start out in the art department, some in copy, and others may even come from the client service side as former account executives. Although creative directors need a good deal of experience in the advertising business as well as a certain creative flare, visuals and verbals alike have an equal chance if they set their sights on this position.

Photography

While some agencies have in-house photography departments, most do not. Photographers usually need large studios with high ceilings to accommodate the equipment, darkroom facilities, and expansive set-ups that they are often called upon to construct and shoot. Agencies seldom have the space to house a staff photographer or the money to outfit a department. In addition, when it comes to photographs, agencies need a variety of styles to accommodate the ever-changing requirements of client projects. No photographer can be that versatile. An agency usually has several freelance photographers that it uses on a regular basis. One photographer may specialize in high quality color product shots, another in fast-action black and white, someone else may do intimate people scenes exceptionally well, while another may be known for reasonable-quality photographs at low prices—a real necessity for those clients on a restricted budget.

If you want to be a professional photographer who works exclusively with advertising agencies, you should plan to have your own studio someday. However, this will require quite a healthy outlay of money to properly equip yourself, and it may take you some time to get to that point. While many budding photographers start their careers as assistants to an established photographer, it is wise to get some formal training before you look for a job even as an assistant. As an assistant you will learn the fundamentals of working with agencies, what their needs are, and how to handle a variety of different shoot situations. You will also learn the business side of running a studio from someone who is already successful at it. This will be the preparation you will need when the time comes to strike out on your own.

When you find yourself growing out of your assistant's skin, but you are not yet ready to set up a fully outfitted commercial shop for yourself, a modest sum will buy you some good but basic camera and lighting equipment. You can then go after small jobs doing on-the-spot public relation shots for agencies, as well as take on those low budget jobs that do not require elaborate set-ups or studio space. This will enable you to begin slowly without getting in over your head with major equipment purchases. Many photographers began by setting up their first darkroom in the family's second bathroom, a walk-in closet, or a basement pantry. Since your clients will be agency people, you will be expected to meet with them at their office. So you will not have to worry about having a presentable studio space of your own when you are just getting started and working on small projects.

Once you become known and trusted, agencies will begin coming to you on a regular basis. Sooner or later you will be given projects that will involve more equipment or studio space than you presently have. At some point you will have to make a decision to either turn the work away and continue doing small shoots or invest in larger facilities and additional equipment. It is important to plan and work toward the time when you will have to make that decision. You must be

FREELANCE PHOTOGRAPHIC PROJECTS

Agencies hire freelance photographers for a variety of projects, such as those listed below. The descriptions include what agencies are looking for from the photographer in the execution of these projects and in the final photograph.

- Catalog and ad materials product shots: These may require black-and-white or color photographs. The emphasis here is on visual clarity. The lighting must be evenly distributed without harsh shadows, and the grain of the photos must be very fine so that product details are clearly visible. For non-industrial products like food, clothing, and consumer goods, you will need to know how to set up attractive displays, sometimes using props and accessories. If the photos are black-and-whites destined for newspapers, you must also know how to print the photographs to best ensure clear reproduction.

- Annual reports: The main priority on these projects is usually developing creative approaches to a theme that will be carried throughout the piece. Photographs will be expected to convey quality in every respect. This is usually the highest budgeted project of the year because an annual report is a visual representation of a company's state of health. As such, only excellence in every respect will be acceptable. You will need to be equally adept at artistic depictions of interiors and exteriors, formal portraits and informal group shots, product photos, and mood-capturing images.

- Capabilities and facilities brochures: The photographs for these pieces must visually demonstrate to the prospective buyer exactly what a company does, how it does it, and what the end result is. Like an annual report, quality is essential, along with a creative or innovative eye-capturing approach to portray the company's most important assets. Creativity is secondary to clearly communicating what the company able to anticipate the growth of your business each step along the way. When you think you are emotionally ready and mature in your business practices, and you have a buffer of money put aside or enough steady work coming in to support a business loan, make your move. If you wait until you are offered that once in a lifetime chance for a large job, and you have to turn it down because you do not have the facilities to handle it, the opportunity may never come along again.

Videography

Everything I said about photography equally applies to videography. It is a highly specialized area, and most agencies cannot afford the space and equipment to maintain an in-house production studio.

Like photography, videography is a highly technical field that requires extensive training. That training should begin at a college or technical school offering at least a two-year program in camera work, lighting, and editing. This should

is all about and why the buyer should be interested. This is both a sales-oriented and image-building piece. You will need to be able to work quickly in a variety of settings, both in and out of doors, with available lighting as well as studio set-ups for products.

- Public relations photos: These are usually black-and-white candids of corporate or non-profit events, although occasionally they are color if destined for quarterly reports or magazines. Any group shots that are required are quickly set up with only available lighting. You will need to be adept at taking quick, clear, straightforward, photojournalistic shots. There is no time for artistic compositions. You will be expected to assertively move through crowds or wherever you need to go to get the shot.

Your role as an agency photographer

If you are going to be working with an agency art director, he or she will explain to you how the photographs are to be shot and what results are necessary for the project. However, you may be invited to voice your opinions on lighting, composition, and positioning. I do advise that if you know something the art director may not see that is essential to take into consideration with a shot, or if you have some input to contribute that will strengthen the creative approach, speak up. But do it in the form of a suggestion rather than an order because, in the end, the art director has the final say. If you are working with an agency account executive, rather than a creative, you most likely will be expected to come up with ideas or suggestions that will enhance the project.

be followed by an apprenticeship or entry-level position with a television production studio or a professional video production company. It is possible to side step the formal training if you are fortunate enough to land a job that will give you hands-on experience in the production end of video. Either way, the important ingredient is experience with the equipment and the application of the medium to the end goal of the product.

Application of the medium is where the discussion of video usage in advertising begins. Most people are well aware that the production of television commercials is a major segment of the advertising business. However, video has other applications as well. A television commercial is directed toward only one target audience—the general public. But there are many companies who sell their products or services directly to other businesses or industries and not to the general public. For these companies, a television commercial is a waste of advertising dollars. Instead, a video-formatted sales tape would be an excellent medium to communicate what they have to offer. These business-to-business videos, as they are called, are now beginning to replace printed sales materials and capabilities brochures. The cost to produce sales videos can be quite reasonable and comparable to a printed piece unless the company needs to distribute large quantities. Only then does a printed piece become more cost effective. Business-to-business videos usually range anywhere from five to fifteen minutes in length. With VCRs becoming commonplace office equipment, salespeople are finding it easier and more convenient to use a video to show a prospective buyer exactly what their company has to offer. It eliminates that clumsy loose-leaf binder or flip chart approach. The video medium is also being utilized by advertising agencies to produce employee and staff training tapes for their clients to assist them with internal management and employee relations problems.

Some ad agencies do specialize entirely in television commercial production, and many of them have their own in-house production facilities. If videography is the area you wish to pursue in advertising, you will want to target these agencies. Or you can direct your attentions toward a video production company that provides direct services to advertising agencies.

Unlike photography, not many individuals interested in working in video will ever set up a studio of their own. The start-up cost for the equipment is usually beyond the means of most people. There is no scrimping on the quality of video production equipment since an agency's clients require broadcast quality for their television commercials and near broadcast quality for video sales and training tapes.

Typesetting

Typesetters work directly with graphic designers giving them input on the overall effect certain type styles will have on a finished piece and the special techniques available that will enhance the way type interacts with the other graphic elements of the project. Therefore, a good typesetter is more than a fast and accurate typist with the ability to operate typography equipment. They are usually well-versed in the principles and methods of graphic design.

If you are interested in typesetting, there are several sources for training in this field. First, if you are still in college, check out your school newspaper—many of these publications have their own typesetting equipment. This is an excellent opportunity for you to learn how to operate the equipment and gain some practical experience. In addition, many typesetting houses are now offering courses like "U-Set-It" or "Set It Yourself Typesetting." These are six- or eight-week programs primarily geared to nonprofit organizations and small businesses that cannot afford professional design and type services. I have known quite a few typesetters who got their basic training this way. Some technical schools and community colleges around the country offer programs in typesetting. The advantage of a formal training program is that many of them will require you to take additional support courses in advertising and graphic design. And the accredited institutions will offer degrees or certificates upon completion of their programs.

An ad agency with in-house typesetting has a definite advantage over its competitors. Since type is a major part of most agency projects, the ability to generate it quickly and make changes immediately can alleviate production stress and client aggravation. Production stress occurs when clients make last minute changes just before a deadline for something to go to a publication or a printer. Graphic designers panic with last minute changes because they usually mean running out to a typesetter and losing valuable time as the deadline approaches. Client aggravation runs rampant when production people tell them that they will miss their deadline if more changes are made. The in-house typesetter can save that valuable time.

In-house typesetting has become more prevalent in agencies of all sizes. Equipment, once extremely expensive and space consuming, is now relatively affordable and compact. Traditional typesetting is also getting pushed aside by personal computers like Macintosh, IBM, and Amiga that run programs specifically designed to provide graphics and typesetting capabilities. These systems enable the designer to produce camera-ready layouts and near-typeset-quality type using a laser printer. Laser printed type is usually considered acceptable quality for newspaper ads, brochures, some magazine publications, and newsletters. When greater clarity is needed, the type produced with these computers can be easily transferred to a disk or sent by modem to a linotronic printer which can produce typeset quality. Because of the expense, few agencies have their own linotronics, but typesetting houses are making their units readily available to those agencies with in-house computers.

This is not good news for would-be typesetters, with the emergence of computerized graphics and typesetting, agency designers now have the ability to do practically everything themselves. And in many cases this eliminates the typesetter altogether. So in choosing an advertising agency to work for you will definitely need to look toward the larger ones whose work flow can support an in-house typesetter and traditional typesetting equipment. While it is not inconceivable that an agency would hire a trained typesetter to work on a personal computer, it is unlikely unless that typesetter is also a skilled and talented graphic designer. Aside from agencies, your second option for employment is a typesetting service. These companies work with advertising agencies to provide them with type and sometimes other related services such as mechanical paste-up. Working with a company like this, you will be exposed to agency people and the work they produce. This will give you an opportunity to get to know key people and become familiar with the various agencies' account work.

Within the last several years there has been a rapid interest in the number of one-person typesetting shops. As with photographers, experienced typesetters with an entrepreneurial spirit and some money to invest in equipment often set up a typesetting business in their homes or a small office. They are able to offer their services to agencies and other clients less expensively than the large type houses. This is extremely attractive to agencies who have clients with modest budgets. If this small enterprise can also pick up and deliver, the shop will soon have a thriving business.

The demand for rapid turnaround in type is essential, but quality and price are also major issues to agencies and their clients. As a result, agencies work with many different typesetters. Some are known for quality, some for expansive capabilities, some for low prices, and others for quick service. While agencies are plagued by and prefer to ignore the vast numbers of freelancers and subcontractors who come peddling their services, art directors and designers are always interested in talking to a new typesetter. Type is needed constantly, and if one typesetter cannot do the job in time or on budget, a designer had better have an alternative available.

Typography

Since typography is one of the more highly refined areas of the graphic arts, you will need at least a bachelor's degree from a good art or design school. If the school has a major in typography, then that is clearly your best choice. A major in design with a concentration in typography should also give you an adequate foundation.

Professional typographers often specialize in the design of typefaces, and some become graphic designers who concentrate on the use of type as the main design element in their work. Designers with a strong interest in type tend to lean toward working for an ad agency that is known for its emphasis on logo designs and signage packages. Designers who want to work exclusively with typographic design will usually have to open their own design firms and try to carve out a niche for themselves in that particular market.

People who are attracted to typography think about type as an art form of its own. They are fascinated by the abstract qualities of type, as well as the power type has to effect people's emotional responses. To a typographer, the verbal or visual message of a printed piece is totally dependent on the type selection and the way that type is displayed. Typographers are usually much more concerned about the design quality of a printed piece than whether the piece can achieve the client's ultimate goal—to sell a product or service.

Copywriting

Being a good copywriter takes more than well constructed sentences and correct grammar—it takes a touch of genius. Advertising copy must be short and to the point, yet clever enough to immediately catch the viewer's or listener's attention in a split second. Then once that attention is captured, the copy must gently lead the audience through the remainder of the message, making them eager for each word or phrase that follows. And copywriters have to motivate each person who reads or hears their message to remember it and then act upon whatever it is trying to sell or promote. If you can write well, if you have a gift for convincing people to do just about anything, and if you have an interesting way of putting words together, you just may be copywriter material.

Even if you are a natural writer, courses in copywriting, marketing, and advertising theory are essential, along with a strong background in English or journalism. While academic preparation alone may qualify you for an entry level position with an agency, you will have a much better chance if you also have some practical writing experience. To get that experience, you will most likely have to go through several steps. While you are still in school, the easiest way to start is to get a part-time job proofreading or editing for a newspaper, magazine, graphic design firm, or any company that produces printed materials. Once you develop confidence, you can ask your employer if you could try your hand at writing some of the materials. If you do well, it will not take long before you have a number of printed samples to add to your portfolio. These samples of your best work will be evidence of your capabilities when you are ready to approach an advertising agency.

Keep in mind, however, that unless your practical experience has been extensive and your samples are extremely good, you may have to start as a junior copywriter. Do not be discouraged. There is a lot to learn about writing good advertising copy, and it is very different from writing for newspapers or magazines. Your junior copywriter status will be worthwhile time spent as you learn the principles and techniques of writing effective ad copy.

With a little luck you may be able to sidestep newspaper or magazine proofing or editing work altogether by finding an agency that hires proofreaders or editors. If you can get into an agency as a proofreader or editor and eventually ask for the same opportunity to try out some writing assignments on your own, your move into the copy department will be easier because you will already have agency experience.

Research

If you are interested in being an ad agency researcher, you should have a well-rounded educational background, and good reading and comprehension skills. Some courses in or experience with statistics would be helpful, too. Beyond that, an insatiable curiosity about anything and everything and the ability to know how and where to find information you know nothing about will serve you well as a researcher. In addition to locating facts and figures to support a proposed ad campaign, researchers must also be able to analyze and evaluate the material they collect. While the ability to write creatively is not a concern for the researcher, you will still need to be able to write clear and coherent reports that summarize your research findings. Good oral communication skills are also essential since you will be frequently expected to present your findings to agency creative and account teams.

If you are having difficulty deciding exactly where you fit in with the many specialization niches that have been described, and you would just like to get into an agency and see firsthand what it is all about, then a job in a research department can be an excellent place to start. It will offer you the opportunity to learn more about the business and at the same time get a real sense of where your own skills and interests lie. Research positions are primarily in the mid- to larger-sized agencies.

Account executive

AEs, as they are referred to in the trade, are the agency's sales team. It is their first responsibility to bring new business into the agency. They do this in a number of ways: networking in business and professional organizations; reviewing trade publications in various industries to determine which companies have been sold or merged, which ones are experiencing growth, or which ones are unhappy with their present agencies. Quite often, however, an AE's social contacts can be the most valuable source for new business prospecting.

Once a solid lead for a possible new account has been established, the account executives must find a way to present the agency's capabilities to the prospective company. This can be accomplished with a phone call, an unannounced drop-in visit, or through a letter of introduction requesting a meeting with the company's owners or officers to discuss what the agency has to offer. This is referred to as "pitching" an account. If a favorable impression is made, the AE may be asked to come back and make a formal presentation that will explain how the agency would position that company in the marketplace and the strategy they would use to attract business for that company.

When an account executive has succeeded in landing a new account, their second job responsibility is to service that account. An AE is the liaison between the client and the agency people who will work on the account. The AE will meet with the client to determine the needs of the company and then bring that information back to the agency account team. When the second team develops the market strategy and the creative concepts to enact that strategy, the account executive then presents the agency's plans and ideas to the client for approval.

AEs are always in a delicate position trying to maintain an amicable relationship between their clients and the agency's creative team. In spite of the fact that clients are the ones who hire the agency in the first place, clients often fight against what agencies propose to do in an advertising campaign. Unfortunately most clients think they know more about advertising their company than the professionals do. Some do, but most do not. As a result, an account executive must exercise extreme tact in explaining why the client's ideas for an ad campaign may not achieve the company's desired final results—which usually are increased sales or profits. When an AE can demonstrate to the client how the agency's concept will favorably effect sales and profits, the client usually gives in. But there are times when clients do not give in. When this happens, AEs must attempt to educate their clients without offending them. This involves a process of gently guiding clients along with the agency's creative concepts and the campaign strategy that will work best for their company's product, service, or image. But if a client ultimately refuses to accept the agency's proposal and instead insists that the agency use the client's ideas, every AE knows that keeping clients happy—even at the expense of producing work that is either of lesser quality or off target— is the bottom line.

Going along with a difficult client, however, is a double-edged sword for the agency. While it may save the agency's relationship with that client, its reputation may suffer when a poorly developed or ill-targeted campaign is released. Advertising and business communities are very closely tied, and it does not take long before word gets around about which agencies are producing which campaigns. Being associated with a bad campaign can drive potential clients away.

In spite of the difficult dilemmas an account executive must sometimes face, if you like selling ideas, if you thrive on constant challenges, if you love people— even those who do not agree with your point of view—you may love being an account executive.

With rare exception, account executives are relationship oriented. Their success as well as the agency's success depends entirely on their ability to pay close attention to their client's needs. They must be able to intuitively sense when a client is unhappy with the agency's work. An AE is, above all, a skilled diplomat who knows how to intervene in a brewing situation before it has a chance to become explosive.

Aside from a natural inclination to enjoy selling just about anything to anybody, account executives can come from a variety of educational backgrounds, talents, and skills. Some are visuals who have worked as graphic designers or art directors. Others are verbals who once worked as copywriters or research specialists. But regardless of an individual's background, the preference for client contact and a knack for relationship building is often the prime motivating force that leads them into the account executive niche.

Account coordinator

Account coordinators are an account executive's right and left hands. Depending on the agency's size, they may work with one or several AEs. They keep files on each of their assigned accounts. These files contain information about the client company and may consist of research and marketing information, clippings of past ads, press releases, extra logo sheets, or just about anything that is relevant to the account.

Maintaining files are only a small part of this job. The creative and production staff lean heavily on the account coordinator for client information when the account executive is unavailable. The account coordinator works with both the production and traffic coordinators to oversee the flow of projects through the agency and to keep them informed when a particular account is about to get active. Account executives depend heavily on an account coordinator to keep track of some of the nagging details in account maintenance that frequently slip by them. For example, they remind AEs when a client is due for a call to discuss an upcoming advertising season, or they keep track of articles about their client's competitor. They may even jog the memory of an absentminded AE when a client's birthday draws near.

If an account coordinator's job sounds interesting to you, you will need good organizational skills for filing and record keeping, along with a pack-rat mentality that will impel you to keep files on anything that could someday be important. A nurturing personality is a real plus when it comes to soothing a frazzled account executive who has been worn down by client demands. As with the other coordinator positions, teaching, secretarial, executive assistant, or office management positions are ideal training grounds for an account coordinator.

Account supervisor

If you are interested in account supervision, you will need to put in at least three or four years as an AE. Beyond that, advanced study in management and team building would serve as a good basis for preparation.

Account supervisors must be good at people management skills. They must also have the ability to retain an incredible amount of information about all the accounts their AEs are handling. They must supervise all the ongoing projects, as they are ultimately accountable for the work produced by their account executives. In most agencies, account supervisors give their AEs final approval on each stage of a project before it goes to the client for review. If the AE and the production people miss something important that was to be included in a project, it is the account supervisor's job to spot it before the client does.

Marketing director

Marketing involves the principles and procedures of positioning a company's product or service in the marketplace in a way that will give that company the greatest advantage over its competitors. People who specialize in marketing, which includes market analysis and research, are well-schooled in economics, finance, business, sociology, and psychology.

This may seem like a broad base of study, but when you look at it closely, these areas are all totally interdependent. Economics governs market activity and influences the trend of business and finance. Economic change and fluctuation can be interpreted and even predicted by understanding the principals of sociology and psychology that relate to human motivation. People are motivated by a variety of factors such as their socio/economic position, educational background, age, and gender. When it comes to developing advertising strategies, agencies need to know what will motivate people to buy or use their client's product or service. Marketing research provides the information that can identify those specific motivating factors.

If marketing is your area of special interest, you will need at least a four-year degree to acquire the breadth and depth of education necessary to understand this extremely complex area of study. You will be required to do an extensive amount of reading—that factor alone tends to draw more verbals than visuals into marketing. You will also need a logical mind to interpret and analyze your findings.

Media planners

The market research used to develop the creative strategy in an advertising campaign will also inform an agency's media planner about the audience a campaign is designed to reach. The research reveals the television and radio programs and/or stations and the newspapers and magazines that audience prefers. It is the media planner's job to take that information and determine exactly which media mix (radio, television, newspapers, magazine publications, billboards, etc.) should be used to most effectively reach that audience. With the proper research completed, a media planner will have the decision-making information necessary to select the correct media for any given campaign. The planner will also know when to use that media and how much it will cost the client to reach a specific number of people. When media planners have collected all of the facts and figures to support their choices, they then put together a written proposal outlining their findings and explaining their choices. The account executive takes this proposal to the client for approval. Occasionally a client will disagree with the proposed media plan. When this happens, the media planner may be called in to further explain or defend the proposed choices.

Media planners should have a strong educational background in market research, advertising principles, sociology, and psychology. Just like the people who work in research, they will also need good reading skills to comprehend a large quantity of printed material and the ability to logically analyze the statistics they encounter.

A degree in media is still no guarantee that you will be able to get a media planner's position in an agency. There is so much detailed information a media planner needs to know to perform that job. That is why so many media planners begin their careers working in the sales departments of radio or television stations, newspapers, or magazines. Working as a sales representative, especially for local stations or small publications, is a good place to start if you have an eye on eventually moving into agency work. Sales experience will give you direct contact with ad agency media planners and buyers. This can be a terrific opportunity to establish a professional relationship with them. When a position becomes available at one of their agencies, you will already have a contact person. By working with agency people, you will also learn how they select media and appropriate budgets and what they think works for their clients—not just what the rating statistics claim.

If the idea of getting experience working in a radio or television station or a local newspaper does not appeal to you, you might try to get into an agency by starting out in a research department where you will not need prior experience. A job there can be equally good preparation for a media planner's position because you will be exposed to the information media people use. You will also get a good introduction to the agency's clients and the markets they represent. In addition, you will have an opportunity to observe the media strategies that are presently being used for these clients as well as those that were used in the past.

Media planners are included in the all business types because ultimately their recommendations have to be based on statistical data, not personal tastes or opinions. They must understand the importance of developing a media mix that will enable the client's budget to achieve the most effective results for each dollar spent.

Media buyers

When a client approves a media planner's proposal, it is then given to a media buyer who will set up a schedule and confirm prices. Buyers begin by contacting the sales representative for each of the selected media and check on space availability. With that accomplished, the buyer can establish a definite schedule based on the client's budget.

In smaller agencies, media planners are also the media buyers. Larger agencies, especially those that handle national accounts, often have a number of media specialists—both planners and buyers. Some of these media people at larger agencies may work only with national network placement, some may work on radio placement only, and others may specialize only in print placement.

To be an outstanding media buyer, you will need to know everything the media planners know in terms of statistics, ratings, and market trends. In addition, a media buyer must be a well-trained negotiator. To use negotiation successfully, an individual has to be capable of projecting an air of self-confidence and self-containment. In other words, a poker face is essential when a media buyer has to play one station or newspaper against another to get the best rates for the client. For this reason, media buyers are also included in the all business category because it is their responsibility to be sure that the client's media budget is distributed in the most effective, economical way possible.

As with media planners, it is rare that a media buyer will be hired by an agency directly into that position without media experience. If you are interested in being a media buyer, you would be well advised to follow the same career path outlined for media planners in the previous section.

Traffic coordinator

When a new project comes into the agency, the account executive goes directly to the traffic coordinator to schedule it for production. They discuss the details of the project and the client's deadline. The traffic coordinator maintains the master schedule which shows how many projects are presently in production and when each of them will be completed. Traffic coordinators are also aware of any problems a particular project may be having and if those problems will effect production on other projects. With that information the traffic coordinator makes the final decision about when the account executive's project can be scheduled.

There are always times when schedules are tight and new projects must be held until an opening can be found in production. This is when an account executive may beg and plead with the traffic coordinator to *please* squeeze in their client's project. The AE often proclaims in panic, "We will lose the account if we don't meet the deadline!" Traffic coordinators need a sixth sense to know when the AE really means it and when it is merely a scare tactic. If the threat of losing the account is real, the traffic coordinator can usually judge which projects already in production have a built-in time margin to allow some leeway in the schedule.

Traffic coordinators must be well organized, detail oriented, decisive, perceptive, and intuitive. Above all, they must have the ability to say "no" and mean it, and they absolutely cannot crumble under pressure.

For these positions you will need to be familiar with the agency's clientele, the production department, and how the agency handles its workflow. If you have the qualities I described in the previous paragraph, almost any job with an agency for at least a year will give you the background information necessary to qualify for traffic coordination. Personally, I have found that people who have come from secretarial, office management, or executive assistant positions seem to be best prepared to meet the on-the-job demands of organization and follow-through.

Production coordinator

It is the production coordinator's responsibility to make sure that all work flows smoothly through the agency and that it is completed on time. This is not an easy job. It means keeping a constant check on everyone in production to be sure they are on schedule with their projects. Sometimes that means the production coordinator is not the most popular person in the agency. A production coordinator works closely with the traffic coordinator to keep the traffic coordinator updated on the progress of all production projects. When the traffic coordinator makes a decision to push a high priority project through production when the schedule is tight, that decision cannot be made without cooperation from the production coordinator.

Before jumping into a production coordinator's shoes, you will need a few years of experience in a supervisory position. I have found that former teachers adapt well to this job because the techniques used in a classroom are very similar to those needed by a production coordinator. With the right combination of compassion and gentle persuasion, the production coordinator can be a steadying influence on the "pressure cooker" environment in the production department. Along with an ability to monitor people's progress and be an encouraging cheerleader, production coordinators should also have at least a year or two of experience actually working in some phase of production.

Often typesetters or mechanical artists will be drawn to a production coordinator's position when they are ready for a change of pace from the possible tedium of working on only one aspect of a project. Production coordinators are able to get involved with all phases of a project. They work with the art and copy people, typesetters, photographers, videographers, and account executives. It is a position that offers a great deal of variety and satisfaction as you see a project come together, but you are not faced with the daily grind of actually doing the work.

Business manager

The end result of all the client service, media buying, creative inspiration, and production is the profit the agency will make at the end of the year. A business manager is the person who oversees the agency's finances. The business manager will alert agency principals when or if the amount of money the agency owes to others is becoming greater than the money the agency is taking in—a very dangerous point. Business managers also hound agency staff people for their job timesheets—one of the more unpleasant tasks these number crunchers have to do. They then compile that information along with other job cost data in order to bill clients on a monthly basis. As the money comes into the agency, they decide how to spend it. Their input is often the last word when agency principals are pressured to give an employee a raise, when they want to hire new people, or when they want to buy additional equipment. Business managers make recommendations on how agency capital should be invested. They decide when an account is becoming unprofitable to the agency and how the agency can improve the profit margin on new accounts and projects.

A business manager may also be an agency principal. This is often the case in small- to medium-sized agencies. The larger agencies will hire M.B.A. types to do the job. The main requirement for anyone who becomes an agency business manager is a strong background in accounting and business administration, personnel management, and financial planning. An M.B.A. is not essential, but it will definitely give you the edge.

WORKSHOP 9

Area of specialization evaluation

Now that you have gone through the job descriptions, the qualifications, skills, and personality types that typify the many areas of specialization or niches that exist in the advertising profession, it is time to evaluate *your reactions*. Hopefully you were able to select one or more areas that you would be interested in as a specialization. The questions in this exercise will help you decide if the areas you have selected are right for you.

Each of the following questions are based on the information presented in this chapter and the chapter before. As you answer the questions, you may have to refer back to those specifics you were instructed to check off, underline, or highlight as you were reading through these last two chapters.

1. What personality type did you find yourself associating with the most?

    _____ Visual   _____ Verbal   _____ All Business

    Or did you find yourself to be a combination of types? If so specify what that combination is: _____

    _____

2. From all of the areas or specific jobs described in Steps Two and Three, which one or ones did you find to be most appealing? List below. As you write each one, explain why you would like to work in this area.

Rating	Personality Type	Specializations or niches that are appealing and why
_____	_____	_____
_____	_____	_____
_____	_____	_____
_____	_____	_____
_____	_____	_____
_____	_____	_____
_____	_____	_____
_____	_____	_____
_____	_____	_____
_____	_____	_____

Rating	Personality Type	Specializations or niches that are appealing and why
_____	_____	_____
_____	_____	_____
_____	_____	_____
_____	_____	_____
_____	_____	_____
_____	_____	_____
_____	_____	_____
_____	_____	_____
_____	_____	_____
_____	_____	_____

3. Next to each niche that you listed above, assign a rating number based on a scale of 1 to 5 **with 1 being the niche(s) you find most appealing.**

4. For each of the choices you listed in question #2, go back and write in the personality type or combination of types from Step Two.

5. Did you list any niches that do **not** match your personality type?

   If so, **add one point** to the 1–5 rating number you assigned to that niche in question #2 above.

6. In the space below, write down each of the niches that you listed in question #2 and list your qualifications for that specific area. (Qualifications should include: education, prior experience, training, self-taught skills, and/or a deep personal interest in this area and applicable character traits.)

Niches   **Qualifications I have now**

_____   _____
_____   _____
_____   _____
_____   _____
_____   _____
_____   _____
_____   _____
_____   _____
_____   _____
_____   _____
_____   _____
_____   _____
_____   _____
_____   _____
_____   _____
_____   _____
_____   _____
_____   _____
_____   _____
_____   _____
_____   _____
_____   _____
_____   _____
_____   _____
_____   _____

7. Look at the qualifications you listed for each niche in the last question. Did you include "deep personal interest" as a qualification for any of them? If so, go back to question #2, and **subtract 1 point** from the rating number for that niche unless it is already rated as a 1. In that case, *do not* subtract 1 point; just **place a plus sign** next to it.

8. Did you select any niche for which you have no qualifications, except personal interest? If so, list the niche(s) in the space below. If your answer is **NO** then skip to question #16.

_____

_____

_____

_____

_____

_____

_____

_____

_____

_____

_____

9. Are you interested enough in the niche(s) under question #8 to do *whatever* is necessary to get the appropriate experience, education, or training that will qualify you for a position in this area? If so, list these niches here. If your answer is **NO** then skip to question #16.

_____

_____

_____

_____

_____

_____

_____

_____

_____

_____

Subtract one point from the rating number you have to each of these niches in your original listing in question #2, unless it is already rated as a 1. In that case, *do not* subtract 1 point; just **place a plus sign** next to it.

10. For each of the niches you listed in #9, what actions could you take *immediately* to begin working on the qualifications you will need? List them below.

Niches	Now?	Action steps I can take immediately	Time frame
_____	_____	_____	_____
_____	_____	_____	_____
_____	_____	_____	_____
_____	_____	_____	_____
_____	_____	_____	_____
_____	_____	_____	_____
_____	_____	_____	_____
_____	_____	_____	_____
_____	_____	_____	_____
_____	_____	_____	_____
_____	_____	_____	_____

11. Next to each of the actions you listed above, write down an estimated time frame in which you could reasonably expect to complete each of these actions. Use the column provided in #10.

12. Which of these actions are you willing to commit to now? **Place a check mark** next to it in the column provided.

13. For those actions that you were *not* willing to commit to, list your reasons why.

Action step	Why I can't commit	Alternatives
_____	_____	_____
_____	_____	_____
_____	_____	_____
_____	_____	_____
_____	_____	_____
_____	_____	_____
_____	_____	_____
_____	_____	_____
_____	_____	_____
_____	_____	_____

14. Can any of these reasons be rethought or overcome by approaching them from another direction or perspective? If so, what are your alternatives? List them in the column provided in #13.

15. For those niches under #13 that you could not or did not wish to rethink your alternatives, go back to question #2 and **add 1 point** to the rating number.

16. As you went through the questions in this exercise, some of the ratings you assigned to the niches listed in questions #2 had points subtracted or added, giving those niches new rating points. List the niche(s) below with a final rating of 1 or 1+.

Niches with 1 or 1+ rating

_____

_____

_____

_____

_____

_____

_____

_____

_____

_____

_____

_____

_____

Conclusion

The niche(s) with a rating of 1 or 1+ represent the area(s) of specialization that are definitely suited to you. If you have more than one niche that is rated 1, you may have to make a choice or find a way to incorporate both areas as a specialty. For example, copywriting and design work well together. If any of these niches had plus signs that means this area is even better suited to you, and that may help you make your final decision.

If you had a niche you were not qualified for but were willing to make sacrifices to reach it, this is an especially compatible niche for you. Because even without the proper qualifications, you are willing to surmount the odds and go for it. This is an area that holds great passion for you. It is definitely not just something you "think" you want to do because you happen to have the right education, training, or experience.

In question #7 you were able to subtract a point for those niches you had expressed a deep personal interest in. The reason that expressing a deep personal interest in a particular niche raised your rating point or earned it a plus is because qualifications like "having experience" and "being good" at something are not always enough, not for the long haul anyway. And we are talking about the long haul as the ultimate goal in how to get the job and how to keep it. That is what this book is about. In the long haul, what keeps people moving toward success more than anything else is interest. You have to be interested and truly love what you are doing. Too many people pursue a particular area of specialization because they are trained in it or good at it. But without a real interest in that area, these people often find it difficult to maintain long-term concentration and focus. They end up "burning out." But burnout is really only one thing—losing interest. When you are interested, when you love what you are doing, you cannot burn out. Because you cannot get enough of it. It becomes who you are, not what you do.

Selecting a niche that is custom-made for you is not just a matter of thinking that this area sounds great or that it is right for you because your education and training is in this area. Instead, if the niche is truly one that is right for you, it has to fit who you are. It also has to hold your interest and keep you feeling passionate about the work you have chosen to do. Hopefully this exercise has helped you to zero in on a niche or area of specialization that will drive you with enthusiasm and passion as you continue your preparation to approach the agency of your choice.

Select the agencies that are right for you

Find your match

You have explored work environment preferences, where you stand when salary and benefits are pitted against potential opportunities, job structures, and areas of possible compromise. You have made a personal evaluation that has focused you on a specialized area. Now you are in a much better position to evaluate different agencies and the jobs they may have to offer. The next step toward your career in advertising involves looking at different types of agencies and what they have to offer that fits in with your personal preferences.

Agencies come in every imaginable size. A small agency can be anything from a one-person shop to a group of ten or fifteen people. Most small agencies handle only local accounts because to service an account outside its immediate geographic area or to service a local account that places national or regional ads can be extremely time consuming and beyond the capabilities of the smaller agency. Medium sized agencies have anywhere from 15 employees to 60 or 70. However, an agency's size is relative to the other agencies around it. In a small city with only a handful of agencies, a 30 or 40 person agency might be considered large by local standards. In metropolitan areas, the larger agencies may have hundreds, or even thousands, of employees with offices throughout the country and abroad.

Some agencies have come to be referred to as boutiques because they handle only specialized areas of advertising such as fashion, industrial, high tech, corporate, or non-profit. In addition, there are boutique agencies that restrict their services by soliciting and accepting only certain kinds of projects. For example, a boutique specializing in corporate image building may only take on high-budget corporate communication print projects such as annual reports, logo design, or identity packages. In contrast, a full-service agency is one that handles all types and aspects of advertising design and development along with marketing analysis and media buying, regardless of its size. Then there are those agencies that will only work with companies that sell their services and products to other businesses.

These are called business-to-business agencies. Other agencies will only handle clients who sell to the general consumer market. These are called consumer agencies.

Keep in mind that size and labels are not an indication of an agency's structure or success. The labels, however, can serve as helpful guidelines that provide some initial insights as you begin your agency job search. I do believe, as there is usually some truth to rumors, that there is also some truth to the assumptions that have developed through the years about different types of agencies. These assumptions are presented here to give you a starting place in exploring some of your own agency preferences. The final analysis, of course, will be made when you do in-depth agency research.

Agency size—does it matter?

An agency's size is not always an indication of its structure or success, but some fairly accurate guidelines have been established that can provide valuable insight as you begin your agency job search.

Guideline #1: Small agencies will give you an opportunity to learn all aspects of the business

Regardless of what you were hired to do or your place on the totem pole, you will be able to observe all aspects of the small agency's day-to-day operations. You will have direct contact with the agency principals. You will find out firsthand what their concerns are in making their agency profitable as they walk the inevitable tightrope between profits and quality work. If you are interested and keep your eyes and ears open, you will find out how clients are billed, how agency price structures work, and what kinds of problems you can encounter if you own your own agency.

When you work for a small agency, you will probably be asked to sit in on meetings with clients. It is here that you will see how campaigns are developed, budgets determined, and strategies decided upon. If your boss is skilled and competent, you may have an opportunity to watch a master in action when a client's feathers have to be smoothed about a project that costs more than the price quote or a creative approach that strayed far from the client's original idea.

Small agencies (from one to ten employees) have only a few people to do all the same things that the larger agencies do with many people. In a small agency, if you are a graphic designer or a copywriter who also happens to be flexible and willing to take on other areas, you could find yourself developing media schedules, negotiating prices with radio and television salespeople, talking to printers to get price quotes on brochures, and meeting with clients to get approvals on ad layouts. A small agency is the perfect place to get the experience you will need to open your own shop some day if that particular ambition is part of your game plan. If not, it is still a great way to get a real feel for the business of advertising.

Guideline #2: Small agencies have a less threatening environment

While the smaller agencies can be more personal and nurturing, after your break-in time the pressure can build as you are expected to take on more responsibility. Remember, when an agency has only a few people to do everything, that means each employee has to do more to keep the agency running smoothly. If you were initially hired as a graphic designer, you may also be expected to take on researching new campaigns, copywriting—if you can adequately string a few words together—and errand running, as well as phone answering when necessary. Look back at Step One, Workshop 3: Examining job structure preferences. If you have **A**s and **B**s for statements 8, 16, and 20, then a small agency may be great for you. But if you have **A**s and **B**s for statements 2, 9, 12, and 15, you may be better suited to a larger agency.

Guideline #3: You have more job security in the larger agencies

Generally the larger agencies (anywhere from fifty to hundreds of employees) handle a greater number of accounts. The more accounts an agency has, the lower the odds are that you will be laid off even if the agency loses a major account.

However, some agencies, regardless of their size, make the fatal mistake of growing too quickly. This happens when an agency takes on *one* extremely large account that represents more than 50 percent of their billings. Then to service this new account they must scramble around, often thoughtlessly, to hire a number of new people to handle the increased workload. Now an agency that employed 15 people a month ago has suddenly grown to 75 employees and moved into larger, more expensive offices. While this may look like a hot, up-and-coming agency, the problem is that rapid growth can cause tremendous stress for both employees and management within an agency. Often a whole new operating structure is necessary to accommodate the increases in personnel, space facilities, billing, and financial responsibilities. The agency principals can become so wrapped up in servicing the new account that they do not have the time or see the need for the new structure until it is too late. If you join an "up-and-coming" agency before they have grown into their new skin, you could well become a part of the shedding process if they run into trouble. Not to mention the fact that they can lose that big account just as fast as they got it.

Time is the real test of an agency's stability. The agencies—large or small—that have been around for over five years are the most stable. And these will be a better choice to target as you begin planning your application strategy.

Guideline 4: You will be pigeonholed into one job area with a larger agency

This is more often true than not. If you are a graphic designer and are hired as an assistant art director by a larger agency, your chances are pretty slim that you will be asked to write copy or do research. Large agencies have copy and research departments for that. You will, however, work closely with the copy and research departments. The copy department will possibly ask your opinions on the copy they are preparing for an ad campaign you are working on. And research will tell you just what images you should be using with that copy based on their market research findings. But that is about as far as your involvement will go with either department. Unless, of course, you show yourself to be one crackerjack copy whiz along with being a superior designer. In that case, you will definitely be asked to do both. Just be sure to ask for more money.

It will also take more time to move up the ranks in a larger agency. An assistant art director will have to wait until the present art director is either promoted or leaves before moving up into that position. Or until the agency brings on enough new accounts to warrant another art director. The same is true for mid-sized agencies as well. The smaller agencies tend to move their people into higher levels more quickly. The down side to this is that sometimes people are promoted before they are ready. For those thrust into this rapid-paced, upward mobility, it can become an overnight sink-or-swim situation.

Guideline #5: You will have a better chance of working on national accounts in a larger agency

National accounts can be so complex that they require a large number of people just to service them. Although it is not unheard of, smaller agencies generally cannot compete with the manpower necessary to maintain most national accounts. As an example consider a high profile, multi-million dollar national account using television, radio, and print media on a regular basis. To handle that account, it may take a staff that includes: a local-broadcast media specialist, a regional-broadcast media specialist, two or three national media specialists, four or five media buyers, three creative directors, two or three art directors, three or four copywriters, one or two production coordinators, a traffic coordinator, an account coordinator, an account executive, an account supervisor, and a secretarial staff of at least two or three. And this is just one account! Multiply this number of people by 20 or 30 other equally large accounts and you can see how many more opportunities there are to work on national accounts.

Guideline #6: A larger agency has more internal competition among its employees

The creative departments may work together on campaign concepts, but the writer or designer who continuously produces outstanding work is going to be noticed. Being noticed means that the more important accounts will consequently be directed to that person. And promotions and more money will be offered, particularly as awards are won and other agencies set their sights on this shining new star. This is good and bad for the other employees who have to work with these people. The good part is that superior performers tend to encourage others to work harder and be more demanding of themselves. Being surrounded by talented achievers is a wonderful way to keep yourself growing as a creative individual. When you expect the most from yourself, you usually get it. The bad part is that those people who have tendencies toward low self-esteem and self-inflated egos will resent those high achievers. This then becomes the breeding ground for back stabbing and a breakdown in the team spirit.

Guideline #7: Medium-sized agencies are the best balance

Medium-sized agencies (from 10 to 50 employees) can offer a very pleasant employment experience, especially for first-timers. I believe that the inherent pressure in advertising is greatest at the opposite ends of the spectrum—the small agencies and the large ones. Small agencies really have to hustle to keep all their balls in the air, and the large agencies are usually handling such mega-dollar accounts that one slip, one mistake, one misjudgment by any member of the staff can be a catastrophe for the agency. That puts an overwhelming burden on everyone who works for a large agency. The mid-sized agencies tend to be a bit more relaxed. There are usually enough people to handle the work load. And while there are still pressures and deadlines, the accounts often seem to be more manageable and the atmosphere more enjoyable.

You still have to look closely at each individual agency. These assumptions are a starting point only. You can find the same problems in large, medium, and small agencies. The most important criteria upon which to base your evaluation of any agency should be determined by the specific information you can collect about that agency.

Agency location—does that matter?

Since New York City was at one time the mecca for most major national and many international accounts, there are still plenty of people who think you can only "make it" by working in New York. But the corporate emphasis in advertising has shifted toward finding an agency with the right creative approach. As a result, corporate management has turned its attention to those agencies with strong creative resources. It makes little difference to them whether an agency is in the heart of the "Big Apple" or northwestern Indiana because fax machines and computer modems have overcome the distance gap. If an agency can develop an image that creates a favorable and immediate recognition factor and sells, as well, that is what truly counts in advertising.

Despite the trend to look elsewhere for fresh approaches to advertising, it cannot be denied that overall, New York City still retains a good portion of the major account activity in this country. This fact alone has to be considered if you want to increase the chances that you will work on important national accounts. The flip side is that the opportunity to work on large national accounts also increases the degree of job stress you will encounter. Some people thrive on living in a pressure cooker environment, others collapse. Consider again your answers from Step One, Workshop 1. What do you need to perform at your best on a day-to-day basis? In the final analysis, it is far better to do exceedingly well in a lesser known agency and later move on and upward than to look for another job after you have fallen from grace with one of the better known agencies in the country.

The growth in the number of advertising agencies from coast-to-coast in the last ten years has been phenomenal. The entrepreneurial spirit among the baby boomers has been in part responsible for the birth of many agencies, along with the acceptance of women in what was once a male dominated field. Although some people cannot imagine themselves working in advertising without being in a major metropolis, opportunities abound for those who prefer to remain in the more rural settings of cities and towns.

Researching an agency—where to start

Some areas of the country have more ad agencies than others. Cities and metropolitan locations support the greatest number of agencies. If you are looking for a job in a city of any substantial size, it will take you more time to sift through all the agencies. If your visions are directed toward a more rural environment, you may have a very limited selection.

If you are totally unfamiliar with the advertising agencies in your area, begin getting acquainted by looking in the phone book. An initial sweep and the first round of weeding out undesirables can often be made based on address preferences. As superficial as this may sound, sometimes you know instinctively that one area of town is definitely unattractive or inconvenient to you. If location is not important, another equally superficial starting place can be the quality of the listing you find in the Yellow Pages. The smaller one- or two-person agencies will often have non-bold listings. If you are considering a small agency, I would recommend that you bypass those that are that small. Not that these agencies are of poor quality at all. It is just that you will rarely find an available position in such a small agency. Unless you have heard that a certain one is looking to bring on another person, or you have seen an ad somewhere, it is usually a waste of time to research and then approach the really small agencies. Many of these one- or two-person shops are either new or have strict financial limitations. However, if you are considering the possibility of freelancing, these "little" agencies are the perfect target. Even if the agency owner(s) do all the creative work, when new accounts come in or the work load is heavy, they do not have the staff to handle the activity.

There is a second classification of small agencies—those that consist of four, five, or more people. These *are* worth your time and research. Most of these agencies are interested in growth. But because their revenues are still lower compared to the mid-sized and larger agencies, their listings in the Yellow Pages may still be the one or two line, non-bold listings. So you will probably have to make a few phone calls to separate the "little" one- or two-person shops from the "larger" small agencies.

You will notice that some of the agency listings have four bold As after their name. This means that they are members of the American Association of Advertising Agencies. That is a good recommendation in itself. But do not be too concerned if some of the agencies you are interested in are not members. Many of the small- to medium-sized agencies and even some of the larger ones never join, although their work and reputations are first-rate. In addition to a listing, some of the agencies will have ads that describe their specialties and range of services. This can help you to more clearly identify those that you might find interesting.

Another source for identifying and targeting potential agencies is trade publications. If you are not familiar with national publications like *Adweek* that publishes regional editions or *Advertising Age,* stop by your local library. If your library does not carry these publications, you can find out which libraries do. Many states also have their own local advertising trade journals. The library can help you check these out as well. Or you can try contacting a local advertising club, if your area has one, for more information on agencies in your immediate area.

Adweek's Agency Guide is an excellent resource for specific information on local and regional agencies. This is a special issue, published annually, that includes listings of most local agencies, their number of employees, the types of accounts they specialize in, and general philosophy statements from one of the principles.

The trade journals run articles that feature the various activities of national/ regional or local agencies. They are the best way to keep up with which agencies are adding new accounts or losing old ones; new people being hired; partnerships, mergers, and acquisitions; and when agencies are expanding and looking to hire new people. If you are unable to locate any copies of trade journals in the library, you can at least get the address and phone number for each publication in the reference section. You can then call or write the publications you are interested in and order a subscription or just that month's issue. Some publications will also send you on request a listing of articles that appeared during the last 12 months. That way, if there is a particular agency or account you are interested in, you can order that specific issue.

Finally, word of mouth is always an excellent way to get up-to-date information on local agencies. Ask friends, relatives, business associates, classmates, teachers, or career counselors if they have any knowledge of area agencies. Be sure to explain what kind of agency you are looking for. If any of these people have personal contacts at the agencies and can give you a name to call or write, that can be a valuable means of introduction.

Keep a file containing a list of all the agencies you found interesting. As you gather additional information about each agency, from either conversations with people or press clippings, put that information in your file. When your initial research is complete, go through this list and eliminate any agencies that are totally out of the question for any reason. This could be based on location, agency size, or anything else you have managed to uncover about each one. Now you are ready to begin the in-depth research phase of Step Four.

The in-depth research phase

Start by making a phone call to each agency that you have selected. Ask for a brochure, a flyer, or any informational material the company might be willing to send you. If they do not have any, take that as a possible warning signal. I am always skeptical about agencies whose profession it is to advertise and promote other businesses and yet they fail to do an adequate job for themselves. To be completely fair, however, before you cast any judgments, ask them why they do not have any information available. It could be that the new brochure is at the printer or that they are temporarily out of stock. If they simply do not have any and never did, put a minus check mark next to their name on your list. But do not give up on them entirely. It is possible that a perfectly sound agency has been so busy making money and servicing clients that it never saw the need to print up promotional literature.

Whether an agency has a brochure or not, once you have them on the phone ask as many questions as you can to gather additional information. Your questions should address the following points:

- Explain that you are reviewing area agencies for employment purposes.

     The secretary or receptionist may try to save you some time by telling you that there are no jobs available. Even so, if you think that you might be interested in this particular agency, ask to have information sent anyway.

- If there is something especially desirable about an agency, and you know that there are no openings, ask if you may send a letter and resume to be kept on file anyway.

     I cannot tell you how many times I have headed right for the resume file when I needed to hire someone. No one wants to advertise for an employee if it can be avoided. Not only is it expensive, but ads tend to attract too many unqualified people that have to be weeded through.

Do your homework

It is extremely important to set aside some time to read through as many trade publications as possible before you make inquiry calls to agencies. First you will need to become familiar with the lingo used in this business—terms like "pitching accounts" and "media flights." It can be pretty embarrassing if you happen to get into a conversation on the phone or in an interview with an agency principal who mentions that their agency is pitching against XYZ Advertising and you think they are talking about the competing team at an after-work softball game. Along with the professional buzz words, you will need to become familiar with the agencies that handle important local and national accounts. Along with that, do some research to find out what the latest market trends are in the specific industries you think you might be interested in. For example, if you have a pull toward high-tech industries or sports gear, then bone up on what the agencies have been doing for the last year to reach these markets and what they are looking to do in the next several months.

Compare agencies to preferences

When you have collected a substantial amount of information on your selected agencies, review that information with a critical eye. That eye should be turned toward matching up the agencies you have researched with the personal preferences you picked in Step One. You may need to go back and review your preferences. With these foremost in mind, look at the information you have collected on the agencies. Some should begin to stand out as more appealing than others. You want to begin to narrow your choices down to only those agencies that are really suited to you. If you are having trouble deciding, ask yourself the following questions:

- Which ones are the right size to suit your preferences?
- Which of these agencies handle the type of accounts you would like to be working on?
- Which agencies have locations that are agreeable to you?

If you are still having trouble deciding which agencies to eliminate, then the informational interview will help.

The informational interview

Call ahead and make an appointment to come into each agency for an informational interview. This is one of the best ways to get your foot in the door and get to know the people at an agency. An informational interview is a "no strings attached" opportunity for you to come in and just talk to someone like the art director, copy director, or agency principal. Obviously, an interview with an agency principal is the ideal situation, but if that is not possible, take anyone who will give you even five minutes. When the time comes, do not take a portfolio or samples of your work. Remember, an informational interview is your chance to look the agency over and talk with someone at the agency about *their work* and *their clients.* This is your opportunity to find out what the job market in advertising is right now. This is not an interview to sell someone on you!

As you make the rounds of each agency, trust your intuition to tell you whether an agency has the right feel for you or not. We all have that "little feeling" we get right in the pit of our stomachs. It gives us an immediate "yes or no" reaction to anything we are about to do. Whenever I have tried to justify a decision while my stomach was doing NO, NO, NO somersaults, I have always lived to regret it. So pay attention to that little feeling. It is your intuition trying its best to hold you back or move you forward.

If you call an agency for an informational interview and are told that they do not do them, do not be discouraged or get angry. Agencies are always fighting the clock to beat impending deadlines. If they were to offer informational interviews to everyone who called, they would have time for little else. So you may have to be mildly persistent.

For instance, if the receptionist is not responsive to setting up an interview or even a brief tour of the agency's facilities, ask if you can just come by and pick up an agency brochure and save them a stamp. You may not get a tour out of the deal, but at least you will get a fleeting glance at the office. Plus, once you are there in person, there is always a chance that the receptionist or secretary will take a liking to you and start talking. Just in case that happens, have some questions ready to ask. You want to be able to take advantage of the situation, but just be careful that you do not come on too strong. Try asking some personal but professional questions like, "How long have you been working here?" "Where did you work before?" "How does this job compare to your previous one?" Keep your questions light and non-threatening. Resist the urge to tell your life story, even if asked. It is always better to play yourself down. You will get a lot further by being interested in others. If you really hit it off, then do not hesitate to ask that person to lunch. It is an excellent way to get inside information on that agency and find out if there are any job openings.

Scout the territory

If you do have the opportunity to get an informational interview and tour the agency, pay careful attention to the people you meet. Try to sense their feelings about the agency. If someone hates the job, it usually shows. Enthusiastic employees will be an agency's best recommendation. Does anyone strike you as overworked and stressed out? Is there an atmosphere of friendliness in the office? Observe the attitude of the person you are talking with. Is that person relaxed, yet businesslike? Once you get inside an agency, look around and take in every little detail. Do the offices look well-organized, professional, and attractive? Does the atmosphere appear comfortable and inviting? Is the employee work space adequate or cramped?

During your investigative tour, try and get answers to as many of the following questions as possible. The answers will help you understand what this agency is all about and how you may fit into it.

- Who are the owners or principals of the agency?
- How did they get involved in this company—did they start it, buy it, or inherit it?
- What is their business philosophy?
- What are the short- and long-range goals of the company?
- What is the company's history with their present accounts?
- What accounts has the agency had in the past?
- What accounts have they lost and why?
- What is the agency's strongest feature—creative, size, service, experience, political or social connections, etc.?
- Who is their competition and why?

And finally, when your tour is over, ask yourself this question:

Did I like the work the agency produced?

If you find that some of these questions are still left unanswered, you may have to look elsewhere for your answers. In fact, even if you did succeed in getting all the questions answered during your informational interview, it is still a good idea to check around and ask these same questions to people outside the agency. If you depend exclusively on agency people as your sole source of information, you are only getting one side of the story. Your best bet, when it comes to getting objective answers about a particular agency, could come from the printers,

PROFESSIONAL ORGANIZATIONS AND SOCIETIES FOR FREELANCERS

Most freelancers join the same organizations that agency people join, such as local ad clubs, the Better Business Bureau, and perhaps the local chapters of the International Association of Business Communicators or AAAA. But if you would like to meet people who are working in the same specialty area as yourself, there are some national organizations with local chapters in most major cities. These organizations are as follows:

American Institute of Graphic Arts
1059 Third Avenue
New York, New York 10021
(212) 752-0813

Advertising Photographers of America
45 East 20th Street
New York, New York 10003
(212) 254-5500

Art Directors Club of New York
250 Park Avenue
New York, New York 10003
(212) 674-0500

Society of Illustrators
128 East 63rd Street
New York, New York 10021
(212) 838-2560

typesetters, art supply shops, photographers, and freelancers who do business with that agency. This is where you will find out what the agency's reputation is out there in the business community.

Of course you will need to know which printers, photographers, typesetters, etc., the agency uses. So add that to your list of agency tour questions. It is not considered out of line to ask who they use for type, printing, or freelancers. These are fairly standard questions in the advertising business. But try to do it casually, when the topic of conversation is relevant. Suppose you are looking at some of the print ads the agency did. That is the perfect time to ask who did the type or who was the photographer. Or if you are looking at some brochures or an annual report, it is expected that you would be interested in who the printer was and if they used any freelancers on this or other large projects. Obviously you cannot stop and write down the names of the vendors or freelancers they might mention, but if you manage to remember just a few, you can call them later on and ask those companies or people for names of others who have worked with the agency.

Other excellent sources of information on your selected agencies are the local advertising, public relations, and communications clubs, as well as business and professional groups like the Chamber of Commerce and the Better Business Bureau. Step Seven will give you more information on networking.

When you have uncovered everything you possibly can about each agency on your list, then you have completed your in-depth research phase, Step Four. This will help you narrow down your agency choices to a manageable number. Once you have eliminated those agencies that are definitely not suited to your preferences, you can begin to focus on the remaining group of agencies you intend to pursue.

Society of Typographic Arts
233 East Ontario Street
Chicago, Illinois 60611
(312) 787-2018

If you are interested in joining smaller, more specialized groups for networking and professional support, check with other freelancers in your area or consult your local telephone directory. There already may be such groups in your area. For example, you may want a group that is open only to freelancers working in advertising. Or, if you are a woman, you may be interested in a professional support group that deals with issues of working with male clients and combatting sexual harassment. You may want a group that is sharing techniques for overcoming creative blocks and job-related stress.

If you fail to find the kind of organization or group that you would like to join, you can always start your own group. First decide what kind of group you would like to be a part of, then draw up a flyer inviting people with similar interests and needs to contact you. It only takes one or two kindred spirits to get a group off the ground.

STEP FIVE

Give the agency what it is looking for

Sell yourself to the account executive

During your job search you will undoubtedly encounter a good number of hard-edged ad execs. To get noticed and most importantly to get hired by them, you will need to know how they think, what they think, and what they look for in a potential employee.

Since success in the advertising world is frequently earned through trial-by-fire, successful people by necessity often acquire an unshakable self-confidence that frees them from a dependence on other people's opinions. I believe it is this freedom and self-confidence that sets the mold from which the hard-edged individual is cast. At this point in their lives, these people are capable of making major decisions without the internal doubts and fears of their less experienced colleagues. They know what is ultimately right for their own business or personal growth. They can seldom be bought, pushed, or cajoled into doing something that will endanger their personal integrity.

The ad execs you will be interviewing with will be knowledgeable and self-assured—real no-nonsense people. Regardless of their personal backgrounds, hard-edged advertising executives are definitely all business types when it comes to their understanding that the agency must always come first.

When you write a cover letter to one of these ad execs, or you come face-to-face with one during an interview, you can be sure that your evaluation will be determined by only one thing—what you can do for the agency. Unlike big corporations or institutions, agencies are fully self-supporting. They cannot rely on donors, stockholders, or foundations to support their business activities if sales slump. Every member of their staff, every piece of equipment they purchase, and every client they accept must be able to contribute to the ongoing support of the agency.

It is crucial that you evaluate exactly what you have to offer in terms of skills, experience, ability, and talent that will translate into billable hours for the agency. This must be done before you send out your first cover letter. Every advertising executive who reads your cover letter will have only one thought in mind: "Why should I even read this letter?" So you had better be certain that your letter and resume give the ad exec a reason to read them by explaining exactly what you can do for their agency.

Our goal in Step Five is to gather together all the positive things you learned about yourself when you did the exercises in Step One. Then we will go back to Workshop 9: Area of Specialization Evaluation in Step Three and review the personal qualifications you listed under the niche(s) you chose as most appealing to you. Once you have a list of what your best assets are, we will look at how to translate them into words that will impress any interviewer.

Size up your assets

Go back to Workshop Two in Step One. Look at each of the work environment preferences you listed in numbers 1 and 2. These listings represent what you need and want in your personal work space. While work environment issues are probably more important to you than they are to the agency you will eventually work for, there are ways in which you can state your preferences that will actually position them as advantages to a potential employer.

Before you begin, it may help to look at some examples. Suppose your environmental preferences involved a willingness to share an office, a desk, or to work in an open office with lots of interpersonal exchange. This could be viewed as an asset to a growing agency with more people than office space. A company like that would appreciate your adaptable nature. If you also included in your listing of environmental preferences that you were comfortable socializing with employees, bosses, and clients, and you are interviewing with an agency that expects employees to spend personal time with agency people and clients, that too would be valuable to that particular agency.

Here is how you could turn the two work environment preferences used in the example above into benefit statements that would interest a potential employer:

> I've been told that I adapt easily to almost any type of work environment. I don't have any problems when it comes to sharing space with other staff people or working in an open office. My sense of concentration is so strong that I'm not easily distracted by the office activity around me.
>
> In addition, I value my relationships with fellow employees and look forward to opportunities that will allow me to spend more time with them outside the office. I find that these times always seem to benefit my involvement in work issues and enhance the chemistry with my colleagues. Clients, too, seem to appreciate knowing that their accounts are important enough to warrant certain social amenities from agency personnel, and if called upon to do that, I am more than willing to comply.

Personal assets evaluation

This evaluation will cover three areas: work environment preferences, job structure preferences, and personal qualifications. You will be using the information we have already gathered and converting it into benefit statements for specific employees.

Work environment preferences

Go back to Workshop 2, Step One, and take the statements you listed under ideal and comfortable work environments, numbers 1 and 2, and use the space below to restate each one as a benefit that would be valued by a potential employer.

When you write a benefit statement that, based on your research, applies to a specific agency that you are interested in, write that agency's name beside the statement in the margin. When it comes time to write a cover letter to that agency, you can come back to this exercise and pick out the specific benefit statements that are applicable to it.

My work environment preferences that would benefit an employer

_____

_____

_____

_____

_____

_____

_____

_____

_____

_____

_____

_____

_____

_____

_____

_____

_____

_____

_____

_____

_____

Job structure preferences

As you look at your job structure preferences, keep in mind that they are often the most important assets you have to offer an employer. They reveal your capacity for on-the-job responsibility and work-load tolerance. They are also indicative of your personal work habits. When you restate these preferences as employer benefits, try to envision some of the demands an advertising agency must face on a daily basis. Then adapt your statements to address these and any other issues that you think may be germaine to advertising agency work.

- Agency work is fast paced with no time to waste on untrained employees.
- Agencies are always up against unreasonable deadlines.
- The parameters of most agency projects are frequently subject to change with little or no notice.
- Creativity is important to agencies and clients, but only if it achieves successful results for the client's business.
- Client needs and agency profits are the most important business concerns in advertising.

Go back to Workshop 4, Step One. Look at your ideal and comfortable job structure preferences, numbers 1 and 2. Take each of these and turn them into employer benefit statements just as you did for your environmental preferences.

Write a specific agency's name in the margin beside each statement that you feel applies to it.

My job structure preferences that would benefit an employer

_____
_____
_____
_____
_____
_____
_____
_____
_____
_____
_____
_____
_____
_____
_____
_____

STEP FIVE Give the agency what it is looking for

Preferences that cannot be turned into benefits

You may find that you are not able to turn every one of your preferences into a benefit statement. For instance, certain preferences (I like working at a steady and predictable pace; I want assignments to be clearly outlined; I prefer to work on only one project at a time; I like having no responsibility for decision making; and I want to leave work behind me when I go home) would not be particularly welcome by a potential employer. While these preferences may be important to you, attempting to restate them as benefits to an employer could be disastrous. Advertising is not the business to be in if you lean strongly toward any or all of these preferences. You may want to re-evaluate your desire to work for an ad agency. You may be interested in advertising, but you might not be happy working in an agency where the demands on your personal life can be heavy. A corporate or nonprofit environment might be better suited to your temperament.

Personal qualifications

Before you begin this section, you may want to know what to do with qualifications that do not fall under the specific categories of education or training. These would include personal interests and job-related character traits which are considered by employers to be important qualifications too. Suppose you selected traffic coordinator as a niche you were interested in, and suppose you listed the following qualifications under that niche:

1. Well organized, detail oriented, decisive.

2. A sixth sense for knowing what needs to be done.

Here is how you would translate those personal character traits into employer benefits:

> I have a sixth sense when it comes to dealing with people—I seem to know what they want even before they know it. This enables me to attend to their needs while keeping them on course with their fellow workers.
>
> In addition, I'm well suited to keeping track of details. I'm good at follow-through and I'm well organized. I believe it's these particular qualities that attract me to a position like traffic coordinator. As I understand it, these strengths are essential in this area of agency work.

Go back to Step Three, Workshop 9, number 6. Here you listed your preferred niches and your qualifications in those areas. Now rewrite each qualification as an employer benefit statement.

Write an agency's name in the margin beside each statement that you feel applies specifically to it.

My personal qualifications that would benefit an employer

_____

_____

_____

_____

_____

Boastful or self-confident

"But . . . I feel like I'm tooting my own horn when I write these benefit statements." I hear this comment a lot when I give workshops on preparing resumes and cover letters for advertising agencies. Some people feel uncomfortable saying complimentary things about themselves. As a result, they have a difficult time with this exercise because they think it seems like a lot of self-flattering baloney. But in today's job market with the competition for agency positions at an all-time high, you have to be able to sell yourself. After all, advertising is all about selling a client's product, and if you cannot even sell yourself, then do not expect a potential employer to have much faith in your ability to sell a client's wares.

You are preparing yourself to present your best attributes in a letter and later during an interview. The best guideline to follow when you have to talk or write about yourself is to explain your qualifications and capabilities in a matter-of-fact, non-boastful manner. If you allow your tone to become at all self-aggrandizing, your intentions will be misconstrued.

It always helps to put some distance between yourself and the personal trait or qualification you are translating into a benefit statement, by stating that according to someone else this is one of your best qualities. Or you can put your personal assets into a context that refers to the specific needs an agency has. The two examples below illustrate these techniques.

> I've been told that my attention to detail is my most important trait.
>
> I believe that my ability to work well under pressure is an important attribute when it comes to the kind of constant deadlines people face in advertising.

If you can separate from or objectify the benefit, you will not be perceived as boastful. However, if you have any doubts about the tone or message being delivered in your benefit statements, ask a friend or business associate to read them, just to be sure you really are saying what you want to say.

Your agency compatibility quotient

The last part of Step Five is to determine the compatibility levels between the personal assets you have to offer and the agencies you researched in Step Four. To do this, go back and look at the information you collected during your agency research in Step Four. Compare this to all the employer benefit statements you wrote in the last exercise. Try to locate similarities between the benefits you have to offer and the needs of the agencies you researched.

You should have already written down the names of specific agencies next to the various benefit statements when you wrote them in the last exercise. Spend some more time now going over your matches again. You will need to match up your benefit statements with your target agencies to write your cover letters when you get to the next chapter. As you review the agencies, pay particular attention to their staff size, office environment, the kind of accounts they handle, and their areas of specialization. Then try to draw comparisons between the agencies and your experience, interests, capabilities, and job structure and environmental preferences.

Once you have thoroughly identified those agencies that appear to match up with the benefits you have to offer, you will know that these are the right agencies for you to target. When you write your cover letters, you can refer specifically to these areas of compatibility. You will do the same thing again in the next chapter, when you prepare an oral presentation for your interview.

WORKSHOP 11

What specialized skills do you have to bring to an agency?

To help you pull together all of your assets in your search for the ideal job, we have one more workshop for Step Five. It will help you identify your specialized skills that are immediately and obviously valued by ad agencies. When you complete this workshop you will have all the information about yourself that you will need to put together a powerful cover letter and an impressive resume. You will be able to grab the attention of any hard-edged executive because you have translated information about yourself into a language that speaks directly to that executive about the only thing that matters— the agency.

Highlight any of the following skills that you possess in either formal training or personal experience. After each skill that you highlight, write a brief description of how you acquired this skill and what you specifically know about its application to agency work.

1. Basic design principles:

_____

_____

_____

_____

_____

2. Color theory:

_____

_____

_____

_____

_____

3. Advertising principles and theory:

_____
_____
_____
_____
_____

4. Marketing research skills:

_____
_____
_____
_____
_____

5. Demographic information:

_____
_____
_____
_____
_____

6. Layout design:

_____
_____
_____
_____
_____

7. Paste-up techniques:

_____
_____
_____
_____
_____

8. Copywriting skills:

_____

_____

_____

_____

_____

9. Experience with designing and/or writing copy for print ads, radio commercials, television commercials, billboards:

_____

_____

_____

_____

_____

10. Working in a graphics design company, printing or publishing company, or an advertising agency:

_____

_____

_____

_____

_____

11. Business management:

_____

_____

_____

_____

_____

12. Office management:

_____

_____

_____

_____

_____

13. Supervising employees:

_____
_____
_____
_____
_____

14. Supervising freelance project collaborators:

_____
_____
_____
_____
_____

15. Computer graphics:

_____
_____
_____
_____
_____

16. Typesetting:

_____
_____
_____
_____
_____

17. Budget preparation and maintenance:

_____
_____
_____
_____
_____

18. Pricing:

_____
_____
_____
_____
_____

19. Sales work:

_____
_____
_____
_____
_____

20. Telephone work such as sales, interviews, collecting information, or conveying messages:

_____
_____
_____
_____
_____

21. Other skills not mentioned here:

_____
_____
_____
_____
_____

Put together a personal presentation package

Get started

You are now ready to take everything you have done in this book and put it all together into what I call a personal presentation package.

As you develop this presentation package, keep these objectives foremost in you mind:

- Make it clear to each agency you are targeting that you have taken the time to learn all you could about them, their clients, and their future direction.

- Convince each agency that your thorough research has revealed a compatibility between your personal capabilities, interests, and experience and the agency's needs.

If you can achieve both of these objectives and do it reasonably well (you do not have to be perfect—just well prepared), you will have a definite edge over 90 percent of the people applying for jobs in advertising. That is a tremendous advantage considering how much competition you will encounter when you are applying for jobs. The important thing to remember is that most of your competition, especially those who think they have unbeatable credentials—like a master's degree from a major design or business school, or an eye-popping portfolio—may not take the time to be well prepared. They think they do not have to be.

Research surveys reveal that employers will hire people more frequently who demonstrate initiative, like taking the time to research and discover areas of similarity between themselves and the company (agency). Employer surveys also confirm that people who are well prepared for an interview are much more desirable than a person with strong paper credentials (degrees, high grades, etc.) or a slick portfolio.

Being prepared means knowing what you are going to say and understanding how your past experience can be applied to the daily tasks of the job being sought.

Thus, being well prepared can be your most important asset when it comes to putting you into that upper 10 percent that gets you noticed and hired.

These are the components of your personal presentation package:

- Resume
- Cover letter
- Oral presentation
- Portfolio

We will cover each area in depth in Step Six before sending you out to make your move.

Put yourself in their shoes

Imagine that you are a president of your own advertising agency. It's Monday morning, and you have just finished listening to a presentation by the creative department for three campaign ideas concerning the new sportswear account your agency pulled in last week. The concepts look great, the copy is snappy and clever, but there is a cloud hanging over your head that, until now you have been too busy to notice. Although this new account will be extremely lucrative for your agency, it will also create an unbearable workload for your staff. Although it is a real pain in the neck, you know you have to hire several new people as soon as possible. If you do not, you could risk losing that new account if some over-worked employee slips up on one of the numerous details involved in servicing this account.

You may be wondering what is so difficult about having to hire some new people. Big deal! Well, it is a big deal because it involves an investment of time which is always at a premium in an advertising agency. First you will have to place classified ads in the local newspaper, several local business publications, and the local and regional editions of the advertising trade journals. Then you will have to spend time sifting through the resumes that come in, and then again spend precious work time interviewing anywhere from 30 to 50 people just to hire 7 or 8. This is the last thing a busy executive wants to do with precious time.

What are the alternatives? A quick trip to the file cabinet where all those resumes and cover letters were filed when no positions were available. If you are lucky, you might just find a good number of qualified candidates for your openings. And if you are extra lucky, some of these people might still be available. There is also one other thing you can do: call some business associates, like printers, other agency execs, clients, etc., who might be able to recommend some competent people who are looking for work.

This is why it is so important for you in your own job search to send your resume and cover letters to those agencies you are interested in even though you know they are not hiring right now. When they are, your materials will be in line ahead of those applicants who respond to the classifieds, when and if the position is *ever* advertised.

This is also why you need to network with businesspeople even if they are not in advertising and let them know what kind of job you are looking for in an agency. You never know when someone you have talked to will be called for a recommendation. These are the two best ways for you to find a job and the two easiest ways for those hard-edged advertising executives to cut through the time-consuming, traditional hiring route and locate people quickly.

Now, back to wearing the shoes of an agency president. You begin to look through numerous cover letters and resumes from your file, hoping to find some viable candidates. If you are in luck, you may find just what you need and save yourself time and expense. On the following page is the first letter you read:

Dear Sir,

I am a recent graduate of the Art Institute of California, and have earned a degree in Advertising Design. I would be very interested in applying for a position with your company.

Enclosed you will find my resume for your review. My portfolio is also available upon request.

Sincerely,

Catherine Cannetti

What is your first reaction to this letter? Probably the same as mine. All of the letters and resumes I am including in this chapter were from my own agency files, with only names and identifying information changed.

When I first read the letter, my overwhelming urge was to throw it in the trash. Here are some of my reasons:

1. This was obviously a generic cover letter that was not even set up in a standard business letter format.

2. There is no return address. What if the letter got separated from her resume?

3. There is no date. That suggests that she has been sending these cover letter copies out for an indefinite period of time.

4. It was not addressed to a specific person or agency. In fact, she did not even bother to find out which agencies were owned by females; she just used a standard Dear Sir salutation.

5. In addition, this letter told me nothing about her knowledge of or interest in advertising.

My conclusion from this letter is that she has not prepared herself for the task of serious job hunting.

I have included this woman's resume. Take a look at it and see how you feel about her as a potential candidate for your agency.

Catherine Cannetti
5761 Sand Hill Cove
Saunderstown, Rhode Island 02874

EDUCATION

1984–1986
Art Institute of California
Oakland, California
Associate of Science Degree in Advertising
Design

1980–1984
Saunderstown Senior High School
Saunderstown, Rhode Island

COURSES
COMPLETED

Typography, Graphic Design, Photography,
Type Specifications, Advertising Package
Design, Television Production, Computer
Graphics, Paste-up/Mechanical Production, Product
Illustration, Copywriting, Marketing

WORK
EXPERIENCE

1986–1987
HL & D Advertising
Oakland, California
Art Department

1985–1986
Sears
Oakland, California
Receiving, Clerical

FREELANCE

1987
Apex
Warwick, Rhode Island

What does Catherine's resume or cover letter tell you about her personal qualifications, skills, or interests? What kind of position is she looking for in an agency? Does she have any experience that could be helpful in servicing your agency's new sportswear account? If you find these questions difficult to answer, you are not alone. I could not answer them, either. The only thing I learned after glancing through her resume is that she took a handful of advertising-related courses. I would have preferred to know what she learned from these courses. She indicates that she worked for an advertising agency for one year after graduation, but she did not include anything about her position or job responsibilities there.

You can probably see from this one example why all of the work you have done so far in this book will pay off for you. Before we break down each aspect of cover letters and resumes, we should look at a few more to help you pinpoint specific problems you might encounter and also see some creative self-selling at work.

Cover letters and resumes

What follows are some cover letters and resumes from my files. See what reactions you have to them as I share my own opinions with you.

75 Bennington Avenue
Jamestown, New York 13907
(302) 555-1234

Ms. Barbara Ganim
Executive Director
Ganim Advertising Associates, Inc.
25 College Park Court
Warwick, Rhode Island 02886

Dear Ms. Ganim:

I am an experienced advertising account coordinator who will be relocating to the Rhode Island area within a month. I have been following the activities of many Rhode Island agencies through the local trade journals, and I have seen several interesting articles that have attracted my attention.

Your recent television commercial for Fairway Motors, using a mime to communicate the message that "Action speaks louder than words," was extremely effective. The campaign's companion, small space print ads also impressed me because they were able to carry the TV commercial's message using only visuals and not words.

In reading the reviews about your agency, I felt a sense of kinship, because I, too, have worked for a small, woman-owned agency, and we also handled several car dealerships. I know how difficult they can be to position in the marketplace. I had an idea for one of our accounts, that was quite similar to yours. But unfortunately, my client wasn't ready for such non-traditional approach to his dealership.

The position I am leaving in New York has provided me with an opportunity to handle media planning, public relations coordination and market research. Since my present company is a small agency like your own, I thought you might be interested in someone who is experienced in handling a variety of jobs and understands the demands a small agency can present. I am comfortable juggling many tasks at once and work well under pressure.

While the enclosed resume outlines my qualifications, it cannot demonstrate my interpersonal skills. I will be in Rhode Island next week, and will contact your secretary to see if I can arrange a meeting with you to discuss the possibility of a position with your agency.

Yours truly,

Bertha Martins

Enclosure

How do you feel about the person who wrote this cover letter? Would you be willing to meet with her? I was. I did not hire her because I did not have an opening at the time. But I did take the time to meet with her because I was impressed with her letter. I thought that it would be good to see what she was like in person, in case I did need someone like her at a future time.

Obviously she had an advantage when she wrote this letter because she had actual agency experience to compare with the kind of work my agency was engaged in at the time. But that is not always necessary. What first caught my attention was the fact that she had taken the time to become familiar with the Rhode Island advertising scene as well as the account activity my agency had been involved in. Even if she had no practical experience to offer, I would have been interested enough to meet with her based on that alone.

The next letter is from a young man right out of college with no previous agency experience. His letter is a good example of how to translate academic experience into job-related qualifications.

56 State Street
Newport, RI 02840
(401) 555-6158

October 28, 1988

Barbara Ganim
Executive Director
Ganim Advertising Associates, Inc.
25 College Park Court
Warwick, RI 02886

Dear Ms. Ganim:

I am a recent graduate of Providence College with a degree in marketing, and I am presently seeking a challenging and rewarding position with a major advertising agency. I am well aware that advertising is a competitive field with few entry-level positions for young, college graduates. I feel, however, that I do possess the qualities necessary to do well in this business, and believe that if given an opportunity, I would prove myself to be a valuable employee even though I have no prior agency experience.

I have been told by several of my professors who have worked in advertising, that my enthusiasm, motivation and determination would be an asset to any agency. In college and in my previous positions of employment, I found myself to be a strong communicator and well-organized. Through my work experiences and participation in sports, I developed the ability to work well with others.

At Providence College and through personal research, I have acquired a solid base of knowledge about how an advertising agency works—specifically, how agencies structure their fees, how and when markups are applied to client costs, and how bottom-line profits are determined. I believe this is information has equipped me to better understand the needs of an agency and to gear my work toward those needs. My research and school work has also indicated that my skills would be best utilized in the areas of account service and copywriting.

The enclosed resume further highlights my education and experience. I will call your secretary next week to see if we can arrange an interview at your convenience.

Sincerely,

Ronald Dempsey

Enclosure

How would you evaluate this candidate? Does his letter hold your attention? Do you want to look at his resume? Would you want to schedule an interview with him based on this letter?

I will give you my reaction to his letter. His opening was weak and vague. Here are examples:

1. His first sentence is weak—his school and degree are not as important as the information included in the remainder of his beginning paragraph.

2. His reference to his desire for a challenging and rewarding position is meaningless to me.

3. When he says he wants a position with a "major advertising agency," exactly what does he consider a "major" agency to be?

Be careful not to use vague references and qualifiers in your letters. Every word you write should be relevant to the specific agency you are querying. Plus, everything you say should be easily understood or explained in the letter.

The rest of his opening paragraph caught my attention and my interest because he told me that he felt he had the qualities to do well in advertising. I wanted to read on to find out what he thought those qualities were. As it turned out, he convinced me.

Those first few words in an opening paragraph are crucial. They will either grab your reader's interest or not. That means you have to say something that relates what you have to offer directly to the needs of the person you are addressing. Since this is a potential employer, you have to explain in the first sentence why you are different from all the other people out there clamoring for a job. You also have to make it clear how that difference would benefit the agency. The first paragraph also sets the tone for the rest of the letter.

The second paragraph of Ronald's letter illustrates how comments from teachers can be used in lieu of compliments from previous employers. Or how one's participation in school sports or any kind of extra-curricular activity could be used to develop benefit statements that you can adapt to a work-related situation. His third paragraph was an excellent tie-in of academic research and course work to the practicality of agency needs. And he ended his letter by keeping the ball in his own court when he said that he would call my secretary to set up an appointment.

Overall, this fellow effectively used the techniques I will outline in this chapter for writing a cover letter that communicates personal strengths in a way that would appeal to an employer.

Now, let us look at his resume. While it is not as strong as his cover letter, since he did not have much work experience, he did make the most of his responsibilities in previous jobs.

Ronald D. Dempsey
58 State Street
Newport, RI 02840

CAREER OBJECTIVES

To attain an entry level position with a major advertising agency, working in account services with some exposure to copywriting.

EDUCATION

Providence College, Providence, Rhode Island
B.S. in Business Administration, May 1988
Marketing Major

Studies included: Advertising Theory and Design, Market Research, Sales, Accounting and Computer Graphics

EXPERIENCE

1987–Present

Brochton Painting and Contracting, Newport, RI
- Painting interiors and exteriors of buildings
- Aided builders in construction and remodeling projects

1985–1987

Cassidy Farms, Wholesale Department, Newport, RI
- Processed orders from customers
- Checked and loaded orders for delivery
- Monitored and purchased inventory
- Trained and managed employees

Summers
1984–1985

Thames Street Parking Lot
Parking Lot Attendant
- Collected payments
- Monitored the inflow and outflow of vehicles
- Assisted customers

EXTRA-CURRICULAR
ACTIVITIES

- Sailing
- Participant, intramural sports
- Referee, intramural sports

REFERENCES

Available on Request

I am going to take Ronald's resume apart piece by piece so that you can get a sense of what to avoid when you are preparing your own.

Career objectives   Aside from repeating his vague reference to wanting a position with a "major advertising agency," I found myself reacting negatively as well to his desire for "some" exposure to copywriting. Either he wants to write copy or he does not. This plus his stated aspiration to work in account services, which could be anything from sales to production, gave me the impression that he was not really sure what he wanted to do.

Education   He listed his areas of study, but I would have found it more informative if he had briefly explained how each area prepared him for a career in advertising.

Experience   When I turned my attention to this section (I prefer Work Experience), I felt he was more descriptive than the young lady back in the first resume. But he still could have gone further to demonstrate his responsibilities in prior jobs.

Using Cassidy Farms as an example, I rewrote what I thought he could have done to optimize his work experience. His objective should have been to translate his previous duties into skills that could be utilized in my agency. Keep in mind that my rewrite is a fabrication of job functions based on his few details.

> Cassidy Farms, Wholesale Department, Newport, R.I.
>
> Responsible for taking customer orders which included: preparation and follow-through on detailed paperwork; exercising rigid control over company procedures to facilitate the smooth processing of each order; performing a constant inventory check to ensure stock availability. Direct involvement with customer relations when problems occurred. Responsibilities expanded into training and managing new employees.

References   I dislike it when someone states "References Available upon Request." The reason is I want to know who the applicant has selected for references. This is my personal preference; many employers do *not* want references at this stage. You must decide for yourself, but I will tell you why I like this extra information. If a person omits past employers entirely and puts down clergy, friends, or teachers instead, there may have been a problem with the applicant's employment record somewhere along the line. The exception, of course, is if the person has never held a job before.

I prefer references to be listed with names, titles, the company or institution that person is from, and a phone number. I am not interested in addresses because I cannot take the time to write to anyone. A quick call to one of the references an applicant has listed can usually give me the information I need to decide if this is a qualified candidate or not. This has been a valuable time saver for me.

Setting up your resume

Put your resume together before you prepare any cover letters for specific jobs. Once you have worked through the best way to present yourself in a resume, a cover letter to a specific person about a particular job or opportunity will be easier to write. Although there are many variations to suit the particular needs of the individual, there are three basic ways to organize a resume. The major factor to identify is what aspect of your personal qualifications is the most important. Is it your education, skill, or work experience? Then choose one of the formats outlined below that best suits your needs. And begin your own resume by making a rough draft of the major categories.

The eduction/skills resume

The education/skills format is usually used by those who have recently graduated from a college or technical school, or who have a past employment record that is unrelated to advertising. Let us look at how it is organized, category by category.

Objective   A concise description of the type of position or area of specialization for which you wish to be considered.

Education   Begin with your most recent degree or educational experience and work backwards. Also list any certification or training programs you have completed and the dates of completion.

Honors   If you received any honors or awards, include them along with the date received.

Related courses   Include this category only if the course work you have done is either far more advanced than the traditional courses in your graduate or undergraduate program or if it represents a discipline that was secondary to your major. For example, if you were an advertising design major, but you took several courses in media buying or market research, that should be mentioned. I find it more informative if the applicant briefly describes what was learned from a particular course as it relates to agency work than to merely list the courses.

Work experience   Begin with the most recent position you have held, indicating the year you began working there and the year your position ended. If you are still holding that job, simply write: Year began (date)–Present. Then give a brief description of the responsibilities that accompanied the duties you performed in each position. You can also add what you learned from each position, especially if it relates in some way to the kind of work you want to do in advertising. Be succinct.

Special skills   This can be a general category in which you can include things like sign language; fluent in French; enjoy writing music and lyrics for songs and jingles. Or it can be divided up into specific categories like communication skills— excellent written and oral presentation abilities; managerial skills—served as director/manager for a five-person inventory team. Or if your student record is all you have to draw from, you can use something like this: As coach of the hockey team, I organized all competitive games, stimulated team morale, developed game strategies, and was accountable for equipment maintenance. Leadership is also another skills category where you can bring in your experiences as an officer in school activities or volunteer work. Human relations is sometimes used as a separate skills area where you can introduce personal qualities such as: ability to listen actively and help people synthesize their wants and needs into simplified terms; or, I have the ability to spark enthusiasm in others.

You can also include Hobbies or Special Interests as a category if you wish. This is especially important if this area of your life in some way relates to advertising or the kind of clients represented by any of the agencies you are applying to. For instance, if you play tennis and one of the agencies handles a tennis equipment manufacturer, it would be important to include tennis in your list of hobbies or sports interests.

Personal data   This is an optional category in which you can add your date of birth, marital status, health, religious affiliation, etc. However, it is no longer common to include this category on a resume.

Military service   If this applies to you, indicate which military branch you served under, the dates of service, your rank, and the duties you performed.

Memberships   This includes any organizations or clubs in which you are a current or past member. Specify the dates of your participation, any offices you may have held, or committees you served on.

References   List three names of people who are not personal friends or family members. Choose people who are familiar with your work-related capabilities and personal character. Again, this category is often not included on resumes. I personally find it useful information, but many employers do not.

The work/business experience resume

If you have been out of school for a number of years and are working, your work experience will probably be more relevant to the position you are applying for. In that case, you may find it more beneficial to use this second resume format in which you can list your work or business experience first, special skills next, and then your educational experiences. However, if the work you have been doing has *absolutely* no relationship to advertising, then follow the education/skills format.

Objectives   This is the same as in the education/skills resume.

Work experience   Set up a chronological listing, beginning with your most recent positions. This can also be broken down into two separate categories—advertising experience, other work experience.

I am always suspicious when a resume does not include the present or last employer. It leads me to assume that there may be a problem. In case there is a problem with your last or present employer, it is better to address the issue directly rather than allowing a potential employer to draw conclusions without the benefit of your explanation. If you are in a situation where you do not want your present employer to know that you are looking for other opportunities, it is best to tactfully explain that in your cover letter.

Business experience   This is a separate category for those of you who have been running your own business. This should also be a chronological listing, starting with your most recent business endeavor.

Remaining categories   These categories will contain the same information as indicated in the education/skills format.

- Special Skills
- Personal Data
- Military Service
- Memberships
- References

The special skills/qualifications resume

If you think your personal qualifications, such as managerial abilities, writing skills, organizational strengths, presentation know-how, etc., outweigh your educational background and even your actual work experience, then you may want to use this third format. Be specific and descriptive when you indicate what your skills are or any special training that you have had.

Objective   This is again the same as in the other formats.

Qualifications   Use this label as a major category heading, then add subcategories such as communication skills, initiative, leadership, training, human relations, accounting, etc. After each subcategory, include a brief description of the particular skills, abilities, or talents you have in these areas.

Work experience   This is a chronological listing beginning with your most recent positions. Include your job title, duties, and responsibilities. You will not need

STEP SIX   Put together a personal presentation package

to add what you have learned from your work experiences, since that was to be the focus of the first section under qualifications.

Remaining categories   These will again contain the same information as the first two resume formats.

- Education
- Personal Data
- Military Service
- Memberships
- References

The creative resume

Opinions vary regarding the use of creative resumes. If you were applying for a position within a corporation or an institution, like a college, hospital, or some nonprofit organization, I would advise you against using the nontraditional approach. These corporate and institutional types tend to frown on creative resumes, believing that they represent a less than serious attitude. But agency people usually get excited when they see a creative resume. It is, after all, a great way to find out just how clever and talented someone can be when you get to see how that person approached a potentially boring project and turned it into something you really want to read.

A creative resume can be set up in just about any imaginable format, but the one guideline I would stress is that the format be related in some way to the job you are applying for. For instance, a graphic designer might create a highly stylized resume, using interesting typefaces and a variety of graphic treatments, such as borders, bars, screen-backed sections, etc. This resume should demonstrate the best of the designer's abilities. Someone interested in ad design might produce a resume that looks like a magazine or newspaper advertisement. Another approach for a designer who is interested in brochures and other types of collateral pieces might be to create a direct mail brochure with a clip-out return mailer which the agency owner could send back as a request for the designer to call for an interview. One time I even saw a resume in the format of a mini-annual report. A few years ago, a copywriter sent me a 60-second cassette tape with a commercial about himself, with music and a special sound track. It was great. The only limit to what you decide to do should be good judgment.

If you do go the nontraditional route, run the layout by as many people as possible to see what kind of reactions you get. If you get even one negative reaction, I would urge you to scrap the idea, because you just do not know anything about the taste of the person you are sending this resume to. If that person reacts the way your one negative reviewer did, you have lost out.

Warnings about creative resumes If you are thinking about doing something different with your resume, be very certain that what you intend to do is interesting, attention-grabbing, and above all, tastefully done. Always plan to spend whatever time and money is necessary to make it a quality piece. And resist the temptation to make something that is quickly slapped together by hand, in an effort to make it look casual or artsy. Also, never resort to crude or inappropriate humor. And be sure you have the skill and knowledge—meaning design and production skills, along with copywriting experience—to create a professional looking piece before you consider this approach.

More about references

Whether you list them on your resume or not, you should be prepared at this stage to know who your references would be. Be sure to get permission from anyone you intend to use as a reference. It will reflect poorly on you, if someone you have listed as a reference responds in a flustered or annoyed manner because of being called out of the blue and being caught unaware. Also, by getting permission from your references ahead of time, you can explain the position you are applying for. This gives them a chance to prepare not only a complimentary response, but one that relates to what they know about you ... and the position you want.

You may want to use different people as references for different agencies. For example, if you know that a particular person you worked for in the past is a close personal friend or business associate or client of the president of an agency you are writing to, then it would be wise to include that person as a reference. However, you may not want to include that person in your reference list for other competitive agencies. In this case, you can attach a separate list of references to your cover letter and leave them out of your resume altogether. Then you can refer to the attachment in the letter.

If you are responding to a classified ad which calls for written recommendations, you will need to ask each person to write a letter to that agency. The most considerate way to do this is to provide your references with a stamped addressed envelope. It is also helpful to include a written summary of the position you are applying for, the qualifications you would like your references to comment on, and when the letters are due.

It is rare, however, that written recommendations are ever requested. Agency people, unlike personnel directors at corporations and institutions, would much rather pick up the phone and call an applicant's references. So unless it has been specifically requested, do not bother asking your references to send letters.

Write your rough draft

Use the following blank pages as work space for your resume preparation.

Resume Worksheet

_____   _____
_____   _____
                         _____
                         _____
_____   _____
_____   _____
                         _____
                         _____
                         _____
                         _____
                         _____
_____   _____
_____   _____
                         _____
                         _____
                         _____
                         _____
                         _____
                         _____
                         _____
                         _____
                         _____
                         _____
_____   _____
_____   _____
                         _____
                         _____
                         _____
_____   _____
_____   _____
                         _____
                         _____

Resume Worksheet

_____   _____
_____   _____
                           _____
                           _____
_____   _____
_____   _____
                           _____
                           _____
                           _____
                           _____
_____   _____
_____   _____
                           _____
                           _____
                           _____
                           _____
                           _____
                           _____
                           _____
                           _____
                           _____
                           _____
                           _____
_____   _____
_____   _____
                           _____
                           _____
_____   _____
_____   _____
                           _____
                           _____

Resume Worksheet

_____   _____

_____   _____

     _____

     _____

_____   _____

_____   _____

     _____

     _____

     _____

_____   _____

_____   _____

     _____

     _____

     _____

     _____

     _____

     _____

_____   _____

_____   _____

     _____

     _____

_____   _____

_____   _____

     _____

     _____

Writing a cover letter

The cover letter is an introductory letter in which you will state your interest in either a position that you know is available or the possibility of an opening in the future. The letter will focus on your personal and professional assets—your qualifications, traits, experiences, and interests—and how they could benefit that agency, based on what you have been able to learn about the agency.

Before you can begin to write a cover letter, you must know three things about each agency:

1. Why you want to work for this agency
2. What kind of position you want
3. Who your cover letter should be addressed to

Never send out copies of the same generic cover letter to your agencies of choice. A separately drafted letter should be sent to each agency on your list. In addition, you should address each letter individually by name, to the person who is responsible for reviewing letters of application for that agency. If you do not know who that is, call each agency you intend to send a cover letter to and get that person's name (be sure you know the correct spelling) and title.

You may think that the position you want will be the same for each agency, but that is not necessarily true. It all depends on the agency and how its positions are structured. With the same set of qualifications, you might be hired by a smaller agency to take on a broad range of responsibilities in a position like art director or production coordinator, while a larger agency might hire you to work within a more narrowly defined job structure in a position such as a graphic designer or mechanical specialist. So the job functions that accompany a particular position title will depend entirely on the agency.

It is always a good idea to call the agency and ask for a job description if you are applying for an opening you have heard or read about. If you are just sending a letter of inquiry to an agency, then simply indicate the general area—like management, sales, design, or copy—that you would like to work in. Then as you detail your specific qualifications, the agency person who reads your letter would be able to decide exactly what positions would be right for you.

Starting your first draft

To write the first draft of a cover letter for each of your chosen agencies, begin by going back to Workshop 10: Personal Assets Evaluation in Step Five. Look at the benefit statements you wrote down in Step 5. There you also wrote the names of those agencies that you found to be compatible with your statements. As you go back and review these benefit statements from your work environment preferences, job structure preferences, and your special interests and skills, find the agency names you matched with them. This will be your working list for cover letters.

Your first draft

Since each agency will receive a separate cover letter, do a workshop sheet for each agency. The more personalized and focused each cover letter is, the more impact it will make.

For each cover letter draft, complete this information:

1. Agency name

2. Specific things about it that you find appealing

3. Any areas of compatibility you have with that agency

4. A paragraph that summarizes those areas of interest and compatibility

5. An explanation of how your skills, talents, training, experience, or pure enthusiasm can be put to use to benefit that agency

6. The position you want to apply for and qualifications you have for it (see Step Three, Workshop 9: Area of Specialized Evaluation)

---

1. Agency name: _____

2. Specifics appealing: _____

_____

3. Areas of compatibility: _____

_____

_____

_____

4. Summary paragraph of interests and compatibility: _____

_____

_____

_____

_____

_____

_____

_____

_____

5. How this is all a benefit to the agency: _____

_____

_____

_____

_____

_____

_____

_____

6. Position and qualifications for it: _____

_____

_____

_____

_____

_____

_____

_____

Formatting the final draft

When you are writing a cover letter, always put yourself in the position of the person you want to read this letter. To do this, ask yourself the following questions: What does this person need to know about me and my experiences to even consider calling me in for an interview? How can I best convey this information in a concise and professional way? Using the information you gathered from your rough draft workshop, you are ready to put it all together.

Here is the format for a concise, powerful cover letter.

1. Opening statement

Begin your letter by referring to the specific position you are interested in. If you are not responding to a classified advertisement for a specific position, you should mention other areas of interest you would consider if there are no openings in your specialization of choice.

2. Body of the letter

Here you would detail the qualifications you have for that position, and how your own personal interests and background experience could benefit the agency. This includes the specialized skills you have to bring to an agency and all the employer benefit statements applicable to this agency.

As you adapt these benefit statements to the specific letter you draft for each agency, try to connect what you have to offer to what you know about that agency from your research. This will show that you have done your homework.

3. Wrap-up

Explain why you are attracted to or interested in this particular agency and, if possible, how that will make you a better employee.

4. Conclusion

End your letter with a statement that says you will be calling your contact person's assistant to set up an interview within a specified number of days. (Ten days is usually enough time for the letter to arrive and be read.)

It is important to be true to your word and make that follow-up phone call within the time period you specified in the letter. Little details like this will impress a potential employer.

Finishing the job

When you have finished what you think is the final draft of each cover letter for each agency on your target list, review it for typos, misspellings, and proper grammar. Then read it out loud. If you find yourself stumbling over a particular sentence, chances are that it is poorly constructed. See if you can rewrite it, by either shortening it or rewording it. The reading out loud test is the best way to find out where the rough spots are in any piece of writing.

Ad agency owners are very critical about poorly written letters from prospective employees, because so much of the work agency people do has to be formally written and sent or presented to clients—from ad copy, press releases, and research findings to media schedules and campaign proposals, to mention only a few.

Finally, read your cover letters one more time to be sure that you have constructed your benefit statements so that they apply to the individual needs of each agency.

Just to be on the safe side, ask someone else to read and proof your letters, too. No matter how closely you may think you have looked at them, this is important. You become immune to the most glaring errors when you have been looking at them for a long time.

Preparing your portfolio

A portfolio, often referred to as your *book*, is a sampling of the work you have produced within the last few years. If you are a clerical or managerial applicant, you will not need a portfolio. It should display 10 to 15 of your best pieces. Choose examples that demonstrate the full range of your graphic skills and creativity.

There are certain accepted standards or rules for portfolio preparation, and interviewers tend to be silently critical about designers who present poorly prepared portfolios. So before you set one toe inside an interviewer's office, review the following rules to make sure that you have done it right.

Rules of portfolio preparation

Rule #1   Each work you select to include in your portfolio should be yours. If you worked for an agency or company that produced a piece while you were there but you were not directly involved in it, do not use it. The only exception to this rule would be something you did as part of a group project. In this case, clearly identify which part of this project was your responsibility.

Rule #2   Include only those pieces that are in close-to-perfect condition. Torn, smudged, tattered, yellowed, crinkled, blurred, or stained pieces are not acceptable.

Rule #3   Each piece should be neatly mounted on a neutral backing of light-weight mat board with an even border of approximately two to three inches all around. It is less distracting if all your pieces are mounted on the same color mat board. If you have a ring binder portfolio with acetate sleeves, mount your work on a heavyweight matte-finish paper. These sheets can be trimmed to the sleeve size and inserted. The work can be mounted on both sides of the paper. Many of these binder portfolios already come with paper inserts. This saves a lot of time.

Rule #4   If you have a number of small pieces to display on a single page, mount them together in an uncrowded and visually interesting arrangement on one piece of mat board or directly on the insert paper.

Rule #5   Your work should be grouped together in a logical sequence. First, look for similarities in the work you have chosen. Group samples together that relate to one particular project or to the kind of work produced by the agency you will be visiting. Projects that show similar styles or share the same graphic category, e.g., direct mail pieces, can be grouped together on one page or adjoining pages; the same with ads, logos, etc.

It is also interesting, from the interviewer's point of view, to include the various stages of a project. For example, you might show a few concept layouts, a presentation comprehensive, and the finished piece to allow your interviewer to see how you would take a project from start to finish.

Rule #6   Always use a proper portfolio case for your work. You will find a wide range of cases from leather and vinyl to canvas in art and office supply stores. Decide exactly what you want to include in your portfolio before you buy one, so you do not get stuck with one that is too small for your work.

Rule #7   If your portfolio is a ring binder with acetate sleeves and paper inserts, secure each piece of work to the paper with tape or glue. There is nothing worse than opening your portfolio during a meeting and having everything fall out. Include unmounted copies of any foldouts, brochures, or booklets you have taped or glued to the inserts, so that the interviewer can hold, open, and examine each piece individually.

Rule #8   Less is more! Include only your best work. Filling a portfolio with so-so samples is a big mistake.

HOW IMPORTANT IS YOUR PORTFOLIO TO AN INTERVIEWER?

The one question that I am most frequently asked by students is: "How important is my portfolio in the final hiring decision?" The answer usually surprises most people who have never worked in an ad agency. The portfolio is often the least important reason why an individual is hired by an agency. But it can also be a major reason why an otherwise competent applicant is eliminated. Does this sound like a contradiction? Let me explain.

If during the interview the applicant is perceived as being well-prepared, reasonably qualified, and possessing personal assets that will benefit the agency, a good portfolio will be the icing on the cake. On the other hand, when an interview goes sour because the applicant talked too much, did not listen well, acted aloof or too anxious (any number of reasons can account for a bad interview; you will know it when you are in one), nothing can save it, including a dazzling portfolio. But an applicant who makes an extremely favorable impression during an interview and then pulls out a poorly prepared or weak portfolio may still be considered a strong possibility. Why? Because personality and chemistry and the ability to use those two qualities to convince an agency owner of just how much you can do for the agency is often more important than your design skills or experience or your know-how when it comes to portfolio preparation. Most agency people figure that part can be learned, but personality and chemistry cannot.

The oral presentation

Your oral presentation (what you will say during your interview) will reiterate what you know about this agency, what you have to offer them, and a brief overview of the work in your portfolio. If the first part of your presentation package is effective—your cover letter and resume—then you will be given the opportunity to present the second part of your package during an interview—the oral presentation. That will be your final chance to convince that agency to hire you. You will not be hired on the strength of your cover letter and resume alone; they are only intended to get you in the door. Your performance during an interview will keep you there.

Remember your personal presentation package objectives. The first is to make it clear to each agency that you have taken the time to learn all you could about that agency, its clients, and its future direction. Your second objective is to convince each agency that your thorough research revealed a compatibility between your personal capabilities and the agency's needs.

If you want your oral presentation to be successful, which means that you come across with confidence as you convey information about yourself and your background and tie that in with what you have learned about that agency, you will need to prepare yourself. You cannot have just a vague idea of what you want to say and hope to wing it. Although some people maintain that they perform much better if they do not plan too much, I tend to disagree with that approach.

I think it may work well if the person is experienced in interviews and has become comfortable in that kind of situation, but if this is still new to you, preparation is definitely the root of success.

What an interviewer looks for

It is important that you know what an interviewer is looking for in an applicant before you begin to prepare your oral presentation. A good relationship between an interviewer and an applicant is based as much on chemistry as it is on discovering a matched fit between the applicant's skills and experience and the agency's needs. So prepare what you want the interviewer to know about you, practice it, and then relax and let your own personality come shining through. You do want to have all the information about yourself and what you can do for that agency at your fingertips, but you do not want to be so rote about your delivery that you look like an automaton. If you can relax during an interview, you will be able to sense if the chemistry is there and if the fit matches. It either does or it does not. You cannot force it. If something tells you that things are not clicking, you might be better off keeping the interview short—not abrupt—and taking a wait-and-see attitude.

In addition to chemistry and a match between what you have to offer and what the agency is all about in terms of philosophy, clients, market niche, etc., interviewers also look for other important qualities. They want to see if you are perceptive, imaginative, and flexible. How do they find that out? By asking targeted questions. I will give you some examples of these targeted interview questions and how you can approach them.

On perception

> This is an ad campaign we did for the XYZ Corporation. What
> do you like about it, and what do you think doesn't work?

Do not let a question like that panic you just because you have no experience is creating ad campaigns. Remember, you are a consumer. Just put yourself in the shoes of the person the campaign is trying to reach and see how the ads make you feel. Do you respond to them? Why? If you think you know why, you have the answer to what works in this ad campaign. If there is something about the ads that turns you off toward that company's product or service, then you have the answer to what does not work in this campaign. Trust your intuition and go with your first response—it is always right. The answers to this question and others like it will not be found in some complicated theory of advertising principles you learned in school. The answers are inside of you.

On imagination

> Our creative department has gotten really stale with its approach to this retail client. What would you do if you were hired to breathe some fresh air into this account? (You are then shown some sample ads.)

This can be a tough question only because imagination is not always accessible on demand. So do not be afraid to study the examples carefully and, if nothing comes to mind, simply agree with your interviewer's opinion that the work is stale (or not) and say you would really want to think about that question. But if you do get a gut reaction or a spontaneous idea, even if you think it is stupid, say it. You can always cover yourself with a casual comment like, "This is just a gut response, but this is what I might do. . . ." Again, to find an answer to the question, put yourself in the position of the consumer who is targeted to buy or use the product, and try to decide what would make you respond enthusiastically. Trust your insights and ideas. I have never seen them fail, even in the most inexperienced person.

On flexibility

> How do you feel about working late occasionally if we're on a tight deadline with a project?

Remember all the questions you answered in Step One, Workshop 4: Job Structure Preferences? That is where you had the opportunity to ask yourself this particular question and a variety of other questions that are commonly asked during an interview—more so than the imagination or perception questions. So you should already know your answers when it comes to questions about working late, socializing with clients, projects that change specifications midstream, etc. An excellent tool for interview preparation is to review all of your responses in the Step One workshops.

Final advice on interviewers

If a job structure or work environment question is asked, you should be honest with your answers even if you know it is something the interviewer will not like. Do not get so attached to getting the job that you forget what is really important to you about a job. Remember, your personal happiness on the job is the ultimate key to your long-term success.

In addition to perception, imagination, and flexibility, you will be asked questions that will help the interviewer decide if you have integrity, diplomacy, poise, self-assurance, objectivity, good judgment, social awareness, and personal warmth.

The most important thing to focus on during an interview is finding out what the agency needs and what you can personally do to help it achieve its goals. Do not think about yourself and whether you will get the job.

And finally, when an interviewer says "Tell me about yourself," what that person really wants to know is whether you will be a good, contributing employee. The interviewer is definitely *not* interested in your life story. So keep your answers brief and relate everything you say about yourself to what you understand (during this interview and from your research) is important to this agency's continued business success.

Know the rules of the interview

The first part of preparation is to know the expected rules of conduct during an interview.

1. Be on time

2. Dress appropriately. If your natural inclination is to be a bit outrageous in your manner of dress, do not do it when you are making professional appearances. Standing out from the crowd is desirable only with your qualifications, not in the way you dress.

3. Answer each question honestly, but you need not feel obliged to discuss questions that are too personal—like your marital status, religion, sexual preference, personal habits, or whether or not you have children.

4. Do not act buddy-buddy with an interviewer, even if you have friends or interests in common. Friendly is fine; familiar is never appropriate.

5. If you smoke, do not do it during the meeting, even if the interviewer is a smoker and offers you one. A cigarette in hand is restricting, and it tends to lessen your professional demeanor. Also, since so many people are adamantly against smoking these days, try to avoid smoking just before an interview. It can leave you smelling of smoke, and that can be a real turnoff to a non-smoker.

Prepare your oral presentation

Keeping in mind what an interviewer is looking for, you can begin to prepare what you want the interviewer to know about you. You will be expected, particularly in the beginning of the interview, to talk a little bit about yourself, your background and experiences, your philosophy about advertising, and why you are interested in working for this agency.

With these areas as a focus, jot down what you might want to say about each one. Your final answers must be concise. You should be able to tell someone in 15 seconds or less, everything that person needs to know about you in any one of these areas. That roughly translates into 10 to 15 words without racing through it. After you jot down your first responses, edit them down until you get within the limit.

Your background:

_____

_____

_____

_____

Your work-related experiences:

_____

_____

_____

_____

Your philosophy about advertising:

_____

_____

_____

_____

_____

Why you are interested in working for this agency:

_____

_____

_____

_____

_____

Review, review, review

As you look back through your answers in each area of the workshop, make sure your responses are relevant to the following points:

- The position you want
- Your strongest qualifications
- What you have to offer that agency

Always keep your answers centered on how your skills or abilities will benefit the agency. I know I have said this before, but I cannot emphasize it enough. So many people come into an agency ready to regurgitate the details of their resumes. Do not do that. Your interviewer can read. However, you may need to paraphrase what you said in your cover letter if you have a sense that your interviewer does not remember anything you wrote in it. Or you may be asked to expand on what you said in your cover letter, so be prepared for that, too. Be careful not to reveal everything you have been able to find out about this agency in one fell swoop. Only bring up what you have learned if it relates to the conversation at the time. You do not want to appear studied.

Take control of the interview

When you first walk into an interviewer's office, do not launch into a dissertation about yourself or your love of advertising. Instead, allow yourself and the interviewer to ease into it, to get comfortable. That will give your heart time to stop pounding and your voice time to stop shaking—common symptoms when you are nervous. You can help yourself and your interviewer to get comfortable (yes, interviewers get nervous, too) by asking some light conversational questions first. Begin by looking around the office. Is there anything about the decor, the artwork, family photographs, or collectibles that would break the ice? Maybe you can zero in on something in the office that suggests the two of you might have an area of interest in common. For example, if you play tennis and you notice some tennis trophies on a shelf or even a racquet in the corner, ask about it. And asking your interviewer personal, professionally-related questions can be a good opener. Try some questions like "How long have you been with the agency?" "Where were you before?" Or, if you are talking with the owner, ask how the agency was started.

Do not wait for questions

Once you have chatted awhile and you sense a natural break that could lead into talking about yourself and why you are there, you do not have to wait for your interviewer to start asking the questions. You can take the lead by asking what the agency is looking for in a new employee. As your interviewer talks about the agency's needs regarding employees, look for opportunities to casually slip in those bits and pieces of information that you do know about the agency, its clients, its reputation, and so on. But do be careful not to sound like a know-it-all. Always try to present your information in an offhanded, matter-of-fact way. Here is an example: "I read somewhere that your agency just won the XYZ account. That must be very exciting." Or, "I understand that you've just taken on the LY sneaker account. I worked in their factory my last two years of high school. I learned all about how sneakers are made, and theirs are such great quality, I never buy any other kind."

These two examples would have demonstrated to an interviewer that you had done your homework. And neither of them were said in a way that sounded as if you had been waiting for a chance to show off how much you know about the agency. The second example is especially important because it tells the interviewer that you have had direct experience working for a new client. You know firsthand just what the creative people in the agency need to know to help them position the client's sneakers in a highly competitive marketplace.

An example of an inappropriate way to state what you have learned about the agency would be something like this: "I've been researching your agency for the last two months; let me tell you what I know about it."

Prepare your own questions

Aside from knowing what you want to say about yourself and how you might answer any questions that come your way, you will need to go into that interview prepared with a list of open-ended questions that will encourage the interviewer to speak freely. An open-ended question is one that cannot be answered with a yes or no. Focus your questions on gathering information that will help you understand the agency's goals, philosophy, and needs. Then you can better decide what you have to offer to help fill those needs. When your interviewer asks about you or your work, always try to make your answers relevant to those agency needs.

Your portfolio

When it comes time for you to show the interviewer your portfolio, talk about only those pieces that you know specifically relate in some way to the agency's accounts.

Try to limit the portfolio presentation to five or ten minutes. There is nothing more deadly than a long-winded designer talking about every project ever done.

Know when to leave

Your time is important and so is your interviewer's. Keep your meeting within a reasonable time frame—not less than twenty minutes, no more than an hour. If you notice that the meeting is starting to run a little late, ask if you are keeping your interviewer from anything important. If you notice that the interviewer is looking at a watch or standing up, take that as your signal to exit gracefully.

Review your personal presentation package

If you have worked through Step Six, you have put together a winning presentation for yourself. You should be ready to make your move. Let us summarize the elements of your presentation package:

- A cover letter for each specific agency or job
- Your resume
- A portfolio, if appropriate for your position
- Your oral presentation

As you worked through and developed each of these elements, you kept two objectives in mind. These objectives are worth mentioning again before we go on to the next step.

> Make it clear to each agency you are targeting that you have taken the time to learn all you could about them, their clients, and their future direction.
>
> Convince each agency that your thorough research has revealed a compatibility between your personal capabilities, interests, and experience and the agency's needs.

Make your move

Make contacts

Now you are ready to make your move, but how do you do it? You can look in the newspapers to see what jobs are listed in the classifieds, but that is where everyone else will be looking too. Your best way to find out about jobs is from the inside.

As the old saying goes, "It's not what you know, but who you know." I do not agree with the first part, but I definitely agree with the second. This chapter will highlight a variety of ways that you can make direct contacts with people in the advertising industry and indirect contact with those on the fringe. Once you learn how to get on the inside, you will see how these contacts can be used to give you the edge you will need to find out about jobs before the news hits the streets. You will also find out how to use your contacts to make your move *before* the hungry job hunters flood the agency with resumes and phone calls.

Use networks

One of the best ways to get on the inside and find out what certain agencies are all about and what jobs might be opening up is through networking. Networking is the process of putting yourself in a position to meet other professionals who know people in the agency business.

Business groups and organizations

The easiest way to begin networking is by joining business organizations in your community as well as statewide and regional groups. Every state and town has a variety of groups that meet regularly for the purpose of networking. You can call the Chamber of Commerce in your area and get a listing of all the business associations in your state. This organization can also tell you who to contact for information on regional groups.

You will then need to call the specific organizations you are interested in to find out when they meet, who their members are (sometimes, if you ask, they will even send you a list of their members), and how much the dues are. Before you make a commitment to join, some of the groups may allow you to attend a meeting to see how you fit in. It is good to do this first, because you may find that a particular group has very little contact with the advertising trade.

Do not go crazy and join every local club. It is not necessary, and it can be very expensive, between membership fees and the price you will have to pay for meetings that usually include lunch or dinner. A few well-chosen organizations can often provide you with all the contacts you will need.

Your intention in joining a business organization is to mingle and talk with people at the meetings so they can become familiar with you. You want to make it known that you are trying to get a job in an agency. You do not need to be subtle about this. Everyone who joins these business organizations does it for the same reason—to make contacts that can help them in their careers or businesses. It is a good idea to have cards printed up with your name, address, phone number, and title that describe the area or niche you want to pursue. For instance, if you are a designer, include an identification title such as graphic designer under your name.

The people you meet at these business organizations will usually become your source for indirect contact into the advertising industry. These people might be the clients of local ad agencies or vendors for these agencies.

Vendors are companies that sell supplies and materials to an agency. That includes paper companies, printing companies, radio and television stations, newspapers, magazines, art supply companies, etc. These people can be a valuable source of information because they generally know the inside scoop on which agencies are growing, which are on the decline, who has been fired, and where the jobs are. They also know who the best person is to contact when you want to inquire about a position within a particular agency.

The clients of ad agencies, on the other hand, may not have all the nitty-gritty dirt about what is what, but they do have power. If you befriend a client of an agency you have targeted, that person's recommendation can carry its weight in gold. Agencies will bend over backwards to please their clients.

Advertising clubs

Local advertising clubs will be your most direct link into the field. These clubs are made up of agency employees, owners, media people, and even the advertising and marketing heads from area corporations, businesses, and nonprofit organizations. Your local and regional advertising trade journals should provide you with information on meeting times and places. Anyone can join. You do not have to be working in advertising to become a member.

The trade publications will also inform you of any other professional organizations in your area that are related to advertising. Some of these include the Public Relations Society, the Graphic Arts Guild, the Film Editors Guild, Women in Communications, and some other specialized groups and organizations geared to photographers, copywriters, illustrators, designers, etc.

Agency employees

When it comes to getting firsthand information about a particular agency, a former employee of that agency is far better to talk with than the present ones, because you do not want that agency to be aware of your private research endeavors—at least not now. It is not that you are doing anything underhanded that could hurt the agency; you are simply learning all you can to establish grounds for compatibility between you and the agency. Tipping your hand about your intentions to an agency's employees will take the punch out of your cover letter and eventual interview when you confidently reveal your knowledge about the agency—its activities, its goals, and how you could help them achieve those goals. So when you do come into contact with present employees, do not reveal the purpose of your hidden agenda if you do have the opportunity to ask questions. In fact, that is a wise rule to follow with anyone until you are able to establish a level of confidentiality. It is better to just say that you are interested in finding a job in an agency and not refer to any specific one until you have a comfortable, trusting relationship with that person.

Networking can give you the answers you will not find in the trade journals. What you read in trade journals and newspapers are often agency-generated press releases which will reveal only what the agency wants the public to know.

Learn the "how-to's" of networking

Once you find an organization or two that are in line with your interests and goals, begin going to the meetings. Be sure to dress appropriately. Prepare yourself by taking along a small notepad (one that fits into a pocket or purse). You may need this to write down the names of people you meet and where they work.

You will also need to prepare yourself in another way: rehearse what you are going to say when you are either introduced to other people at these meetings or when you introduce yourself. Yes, introduce yourself! In most of these organizations there is no formal procedure for introducing new members. You will be expected to mingle on your own and introduce yourself.

Most of these meetings will begin with a coffee or cocktail hour, during which you can walk around and decide who looks friendly and open to talking with a stranger. Begin at one end of the room and take a visual survey of everyone there. Some people will be standing alone. Those people are usually the easiest to approach because they too may be new members and feeling a bit adrift. Then there are the little pockets or groups of people. Some of these groups may be difficult to break into if they are made up of friends who are involved in a personal or intimate conversation. Study the groups carefully before you intrude.

The best way to access the approachability of a group is to move slowly through the crowd and stop close enough to overhear what each one is talking about. If it seems to be of a non-intimate nature, wait for a natural break in the conversation and try to position yourself in a way that makes it easy to turn and casually strike up a conversation with one of the group members. You could interject something related to what you overhead in the conversation that was of interest to you. For example, "Excuse me, but I thought I heard you mention that new agency that just opened last week. Do you know anything about its founders?" However, do be careful that you do not interject with a gossipy or prying question. You could also begin a conversation with a personal (but not too personal) question like, "You look so familiar. I've been trying to figure out where I might have seen you before."

Once you manage to break into a group or strike up an individual conversation, you should then briefly state why you have joined this organization or why you are thinking about joining it. Then stop talking about yourself and shift your attention to the other person or people you are meeting. Ask what each of them does and why they are here. If this type of interaction is uncomfortable for you, practice beforehand in front of a mirror, while you are driving, or with a friend. Do it until it becomes easy and natural. It is important to make a good first impression. After all, you may just find yourself saying hello to the personnel director of your favorite advertising agency.

One word of advice: prepare more questions to ask other people than material about yourself. People love to talk about themselves. If you can focus more attention on other people than on yourself, they will go away thinking that you are terrific. Plus, if you can keep people talking about themselves, that keeps the spotlight off you for a while. That could be important if you are a little nervous and need time to compose yourself, catch your breath, and get comfortable. On the other hand, be sensitive to the person you are plying with chatty questions. If you sense reluctance, you may need to offer a polite, "Excuse me, I'll talk to you later," and move on to other more receptive contacts.

Networking with friends and relatives

You can also network right in your own backyard. Think about everyone you already know—friends and relatives. Is there anyone who in any way may be associated with advertising? It could be someone whose golfing partner is an agency account executive, or someone who works for a radio or a television station or a newspaper or a magazine who might have a personal relationship with people in the agency business. There may even be someone in your circle of acquaintances who uses the services of advertising professionals. Ask around. You may be surprised at the connections you will find.

If you discover a few potential contacts, make a date to get together. Go out to lunch and plan to pay for it. These people have the potential to help you, so you do not want to give them the impression that you are taking their time for granted. Even close friends and relatives should be treated with professional courtesy. Tell each person you meet with exactly what your goals are and which agencies you have identified as compatible with you and why. Find out who they know in advertising and what they know about specific agencies and the industry in general. See if they can introduce you to anyone who would be willing to give you more information. Also, ask if they would mind making a call to one of these people to help you get your resume and cover letter to the appropriate person. Be sure to ask each of your contacts if you are imposing by asking for personal assistance. Always preface your request with the acknowledgment that if they feel uncomfortable in any way about making a phone call, that you understand perfectly. If any of your contacts are hesitant about calling someone for you, ask if they would mind if you called the person yourself and used their name. This can sometimes be just as effective, and it certainly takes your person off the hook.

Send a thank you note to every person who helps you make a contact or gives you advice, recommendations, or leads. It is also thoughtful to keep these people informed of your progress—when you land an interview or get a job offer.

It probably will not happen overnight, but with persistence, several meetings, and perhaps even follow-up lunches under your belt, you are likely to make some significant contacts. Keep in mind that you may not get a job from these contacts, but I can guarantee you that they will play an important role in your professional life at some time in the future. This is the reason that networking never ends. It will become an important part of your professional life no matter how high you rise in the advertising community. Always remember that you cannot have too many friends in business. Of course, the other thing to always remember is that you have to be a friend to have a friend.

Ready, set, go

When your resume and cover letters are ready to go out, you can begin sending them to each agency on your list whether there is an available position or not. It is important just to get your materials out there because the nature of agency business is *change*. New accounts are added every day, and that often creates an immediate need for new people. Thus having your resume on file will give you an edge over any applicants who respond to an ad when a position is advertised, if the position is ever advertised at all.

Once you have sent your cover letters and resumes out, be sure to follow up each one with a phone call to see that your materials have arrived. During that call, ask if you can arrange an interview with the person you addressed the letter to. You may be told on the phone by the assistant or the receptionist that the agency is not hiring right now and your contact person is not accepting appointments for interviews. If that happens, ask if you could come in for an agency tour (if you have not done that with this agency yet) with someone in the department you want to work in. If you are still put off, then ask the person you are speaking with to please keep your resume on file in the event that a position opens up. Then you can call back every six months or so, just to check on the status of available openings.

Classified ads

As I mentioned earlier, classified ads are not the best way to find out about an opening, but do not ignore them. The Sunday classified section in your local newspaper will be your best bet. Sunday papers have the highest weekly readership, so many agencies place ads to run only on Sundays. It is also a good investment to get a subscription to any local advertising magazines or business newspapers. Not only will you benefit from keeping up with the latest business community news, but most of these publications have classified sections. When an agency does have a position to fill, often the owner(s) will not even bother with the local paper but will instead place ads in local and regional advertising journals and business newspapers.

When you decide to respond to an ad, run through your list of network contacts to see if anyone you know has any connections at this agency. Anything you can do to make your cover letter and resume stand out from the many others that will come in at the same time will help.

Many classified ads specifically state that an applicant must send in a resume, and no phone calls will be accepted. In that case, it would be inappropriate to say in your cover letter that you will call to set up an appointment. You will just have to sit tight and wait to be called in for an interview.

Persistence is the key

Even if you get one of these dreaded letters back that says, "Thank you for your interest in our agency, but the position you inquired about has been filled," do not let that stand in your way. Just keep trying. Keep calling back every few months to see what is happening—if there are any new openings. And, if there is any way you can do it, try to get into the agency to meet with someone—anyone. If you cannot get to the top dog, take the underdog.

Kind, gentle, and thoughtful persistence will take you further than all the portfolios and degrees in the world. Persistence does not mean hounding people, it means making yourself available, coming back, and never giving up. Even if an agency does not have a position today, they will some day, and if you keep trying, they will not forget you.

Know how interviews work

If you have faithfully followed the advice in this book, those "sorry, we've filled that position" letters will be few and far between. What you will get is plenty of invitations to come in for an interview. There are several different types of interviews which you might encounter. Knowing how these interviews work and why an agency might opt to use one type rather than another will help you gear your oral presentation to the type of interview you might face.

One-on-one interview

This is the most typical kind of interview format. You will meet with the person who does the hiring. This is generally the agency president or owner. While you may have an opportunity to meet members of the department you will be working in – and their reaction to you will certainly carry some weight – the final decision rests entirely with your interviewer.

Smaller agencies in particular use this style of interview, because it is most efficient—for the interviewer and you. You will not have to worry about impressing a lot of people. And your interviewer will not have to be concerned with other people's opinions of you.

The stepladder interview

This process begins with the department head who will be your supervisor. If the agency is very large, it may begin with a personnel director and then move up to the department head. If you do well in the first interview, you will be invited back for a second interview with one or more members of the management team who oversee the department. If you fare well in that arena, you will be brought in to meet with the agency principals or owners. The larger the agency, the more levels you will have to pass through before a final vote is taken.

This type of interview might take place during a single morning, or it could stretch out over several days or weeks. It all depends on how many people you will have to meet with, when these people are available, and how many other candidates they have to interview. While this system is not as efficient as the one-on-one interview, it does get all of the people who will have to work with you involved in evaluating your ability to contribute to the agency. If there is a problem between you and a key person at the agency, in either personal chemistry, philosophy, or working style, chances are that it will be sensed during one of these stepladder interviews.

To prepare for a stepladder interview, remember that you will need to adapt your answers and comments to the particular concerns of the person(s) you are meeting with. For example, when you meet with the department head, you will be predominantly interested in the concerns and needs of that person and that department. When you are talking with management, address their concerns. Be sure to answer each person's questions fully and completely, even though you may have said exactly the same thing to someone else in the agency the day before. Do not assume that these people have shared what you said with each other.

Group or committee interviews

Even though this interview format is fairly rare, it does happen. You may be asked to come in for an interview with a hiring group or committee. It will most often take place in a conference room at a large table in which you will meet with these other people—usually the same people you would meet during a stepladder interview, only here you see them all together.

Some agencies like to use the group structure because it is efficient in that it brings all of the appropriate people together to meet with you at one time. It is also an excellent way to see how you react to a group of different individuals with varying concerns and attitudes. This is probably the best way to see how you would perform during a group meeting with a client and their staff or during an agency presentation to a client presentation committee. Since presentations are the way agencies get 60 percent of their business, it may be important for your interviewers to know ahead of time how well you would stand up during the pressure of a group encounter if the position you are being considered for involves participation in presentations.

You need to remember to make eye contact with each member of the group as you speak. Some people make the mistake of picking one person and addressing everything they say to that person.

The callback interview

If your one on one meeting with an agency owner was successful, but there were other applicants after you who were equally impressive, you may be called back for a second interview. During this time you may be asked questions that were raised when the agency head met with one of these other people. Or you may be asked more in-depth questions.

Get past the nervous jitters

Everyone gets a little nervous before and during an interview. It is normal, and it is also helpful because it triggers a flow of adrenalin which will heighten your mental clarity. But when a case of nerves gets out of control, and you are actually incapacitated in some way, this can be a serious problem. Some people get so frightened at the thought of meeting new people or talking about themselves that they feel faint or short of breath or their hands shake uncontrollably. This can be embarrassing and can make you appear incompetent. Those people who are severely effected by nervousness often believe they have no control over the situation. But the fact is they do; we all do.

The solution boils down to choice. You have two choices: to be nervous or not to be nervous. If you choose *not* to be nervous, you will stop dwelling on failure and being overcome by your nerves, which will cause you to be even more upset and nervous. Instead you will be focusing your attention on finding ways to abate your nervousness. Whatever you focus your attention on—whatever you think about constantly—is exactly what will happen. If you focus on using certain techniques to diffuse your nerves and to calm yourself, you will not have time to worry. If you put your energy into what you want to say during an interview and what questions you want to ask, instead of being immobilized by your fear, you will be well prepared and feel confident. We can sabotage ourselves from doing the very thing that we need to do to have a successful interview by focusing on what could happen if our nerves get out of control.

Mental rehearsal is critical

Once you choose *not* to be nervous, there are techniques you can use to dilute your nervousness down to a manageable level. The first one is mental rehearsal. It has been proven during a series of research experiments that whatever a person visualizes or imagines will be recorded in the mind's memory in exactly the same way that an actual experience is recorded.

High school basketball players were divided into three groups of ten each. For a period of ten days, one of the groups had to spend 30 minutes each day practicing lay-up shots on the court. Another group had to spend 30 minutes visualizing themselves on the court, standing in front of the basket, and throwing lay-up shots. They did this each night before they went to sleep. The third group did nothing for ten days. At the end of this experiment, the group that actually practiced the lay-up shots and the group that visualized themselves practicing both experienced a 97 percent increase in their ability to make the shot when they returned to the court. The group that did nothing experienced a decrease in their shooting abilities. This same experiment was performed over and over for several years with exactly the same results. The group that visualized did as well as the group that actually went out on the court and practiced each day.

So you can see just how powerful a tool visualization can be. That is why people who keep thinking about how nervous they will be during an interview find that the prophesy comes true. Their minds have already recorded an image of themselves being nervous. So when the real situation comes about, their bodies perform based on a preconditioned memory—a memory of being nervous.

But you can create a different preconditioned memory. When you have your oral presentation prepared, set aside 30 minutes each day before your interview and go to a quiet place. Sit down, close your eyes, and visualize yourself walking into the agency building and then the main office.

If you are not familiar with the agency's building, take a little trip and have a look. Actually go inside the building and look around. Go into the agency so that you can have a picture in your mind of what the place looks like. Do not hesitate to tell the receptionist that you just came by to be sure you had your directions straight before your interview.

Then when you visualize, see yourself sitting down in the reception area and taking several deep breaths before you are called into your interviewer's office. See yourself walk into the office and envision what you will say at that time. Go through the small talk for the initial part of the interview. Then imagine yourself sitting down and feeling really relaxed and comfortable, as if you were talking with an old friend. Then picture in your mind the remainder of the interview, what the person might ask you, and how you will answer each question. Hear and feel yourself speaking clearly and with complete confidence.

The more detail you can bring to your visualization, the stronger your memory record will be. This memory record will kick into play when you go into the real interview. And just like anything that you have done over and over, being calm, comfortable, and knowing just what you are going to say will become automatic. Your mind and body will move cooperatively together to repeat the same pattern of movements, thoughts, energy, and calm confidence, since that will be a major part of your visualization and memory. If you can do this for a week or ten days, you will be astounded by the results.

Distract yourself

One of the main reasons for preparing small talk questions to ask your interviewer when you first walk into the office is to create a distraction for yourself. You see, nervousness is just like the hiccups—once it starts it is hard to stop it. You have probably noticed that when you try to get rid of the hiccups, it never works. What you are really doing is focusing more attention on them. Remember, what you focus your attention on will keep happening. But when you get distracted and begin doing something else that takes your mind off your hiccups, then they are gone.

Nervousness works in exactly the same way. If you can distract yourself for as little as 30 seconds, doing something that requires you to take your attention away from yourself, your nervousness will disappear. It really works!

When you walk into an interviewer's office, focus all of your attention on that person. Really look at this person. Take in every detail of the office, then start asking a few questions about the agency, or your interviewer's background, or the climate of the ad business right now. Remember, people love to talk about themselves. And when you ask these questions, really listen to the answers and look for an opportunity to formulate another question from the answer. You will get so wrapped up in paying attention to your interviewer that you will totally forget about being nervous. Once you break the nervous pattern, it rarely comes back. If it does, simply ask another question and distract yourself again.

"What, me work for nothing?"

There will be times when you will be asked to come into an agency for an interview even though there are no positions available. If you go and you find yourself feeling like you would give your eye teeth to work there, what can you do?

Almost no one can resist someone who offers to come in and work for nothing, or close to it. I know what you are thinking, that I must be crazy to even suggest this. But if you are in a position where you can afford to do this for a limited period of time, like three months, this could be the shortest step to a big leap forward. Why?

Look at it this way. According to national statistics recorded during the last three years, most people who are qualified but inexperienced and trying to break into a new field are spending anywhere from six to nine months trying to locate a suitable position. What if it takes you that long to find a job for yourself? You may think that you are different, and certainly *you* will find something within a month or two at the most. Maybe, maybe not. If you can survive financially for two or even three months without a paying position, you might find it advantageous to offer to work for the agency of your choice for free or for minimum wage. If that is impossible for you, but getting a job with this agency is worth taking a salary cut for awhile, find out what most people with your qualifications and background are getting in local ad agencies. Then offer yourself at half that to come in and learn the ropes. But offer yourself for only a limited time period, such as three months at the most. And put that in writing. This method will not guarantee a full-time job offer, but the odds of that happening are in your favor. If you are not offered a salaried position at the end of your 3-month stint, you at least have gained experience that may help you with the next position you go after.

Job openings are hard to find, especially for anyone without the practical, hands-on experience that is so important to an ad agency when no one has the time to train a new employee. So coming in for a specified period of time at half pay or even no pay—if the half price offer is turned down—can be your quickest ticket to a full-time, full-salary position. And while the other jobless people are still out there pounding the pavement four months later, you will be sitting pretty with not just a job, but a job in the agency of your choice.

Warning: If you decide to do this, it is crucial that you are totally clear with the agency principal(s) that you are making this offer because, although you realize you have no prior agency experience to offer, you are willing to take responsibility for your own training. Then try to negotiate a price that you can both live with. Begin with half salary, and if that is rejected, go to minimum wage if you can afford it. Then as a last resort, again only if you can manage it financially, offer your services for free. But do explain carefully that this is only a limited offer of 60 days or 90 days.

Stick with 90 days as your limit. Do not allow yourself to go beyond that. And absolutely refuse to do this if the owner(s) are not willing to sign an agreement stating your intentions and the length of time you will make this offer available. Keep in mind that you may not be able to get them to promise you a full-time position when your offer ends. That will all depend on how irreplaceable you make yourself during your trial period.

Make the right decision

Imagine that you receive a phone call saying, "We'd like to offer you the job." What a feeling that would be! And if this happens, and it will, what is the first thing you should do? You probably think you should say yes, right then and there, before they change their minds. Am I right? Well, if that is what you are thinking, you are wrong! No matter how tempting it may be, tell whoever calls you that you will need time to think it over and you will get back to them in a day or two. (Do not push your luck by trying to take a week to decide.)

What do you have to think about? After all, this is a job made in heaven with the agency of your dreams. Is it? Maybe, but first look carefully at everything that you know about this position and everything that you do not know.

What is the exact position?

Make sure you know what you are being hired for. If you were responding to a classified ad, then you should have a fairly good idea of what you are being hired to do. If you went in for an interview when there was no specific position available, did your interviewer or the person who called to offer you the job explain what you would be doing? If you write copy but told your interviewer that you wanted to work in the copy department, you could just find yourself working in the copy department as an errand person or a proofreader. Would you be happy doing that?

If you are at all vague on what you might be hired to do, the first thing you will have to do is to ask for a job description—this could be verbal or written. A written job description is always preferable, but if the agency does not have written job descriptions, and many do not, then you might irritate them if you insist on one. If the job description is given to you verbally, be sure to listen to it carefully and take notes. Then decide if this is exactly what you want to do and would be happy doing. If not, you will have to talk with your interviewer and try to negotiate the terms of your position. But do it before you say yes. Do not think that you can wait until you get in there and try to change things.

How about salary?

It is certainly not the first question you want to ask during an interview, but if the meeting with your interviewer goes well, it is definitely appropriate to inquire about the salary and benefits package. If your interviewer says something like, "Oh, it's in the mid- to upper-twenties, but we can discuss that later," when you are offered the job, the time for *later* has come.

Always, before you say yes, ask what is being offered in salary and benefits. When you are given an answer, do not think that the offer is written in stone. There is still time to negotiate for more if you need it.

The first thing you need to do before you begin negotiating is to figure out how much money you need to live comfortably and how much you want in order to be happy. Are those amounts the same or different? If they are different, can you realistically expect to get your salary offer up to that level? Trust your intuition to be your guide. If you hear that little voice inside of you saying, "What, are you crazy? If you tell them you want that much, they'll tell you to take a leap." Listen to that voice. Also, check with your network contacts and see what the average salary and benefits package is in a comparable agency for someone with your experience. Then if you believe you have been shot a low-ball figure, make a counteroffer and see what happens. The agency people may make you another offer of half the increase you are requesting. Can you live with that? Also, be prepared for the possibility that your counteroffer will be turned down altogether. In that case, you can say you will accept the position at that salary with the understanding that you could have a salary review in six months. That, too, may be accepted or rejected.

Now you will have to decide if you can accept the initial salary quoted and the benefits that go with it. If this is your first job in advertising, it may not be prudent to be extremely fussy or stubborn. But on the other hand, you do not want to put yourself in a position to be taken advantage of. Once again, trust that inner guidance to lead you to the right answer.

How about benefits?

If you are young and just getting started, you may not think that a health insurance policy or paid vacation days are important, but they are. If anything happens to you—an illness or an accident—medical costs are outrageous. Paying for one visit to an emergency room with a broken leg and a cast can cost a month's salary or more. Health insurance is important; do not short change yourself there. It is sometimes better to accept a little bit less in salary in return for a better benefits package. And you do not have to pay income tax on benefits.

In addition to health insurance, paid vacation time and paid sick days can be important. You may also be able to negotiate tuition reimbursement, particularly with some of the larger agencies.

Conflicts with your personal life or integrity

If you are not sure, go back to Step One and review all the questions you rated concerning work environment preferences, job structure preferences, and your values and attitudes about money. Then think back to your interview. Did anything happen or was anything said that would lead you to believe that there would be any conflicts with any of your preferences in these areas? You may not remember at first but when you look at the questions in Step One, you may notice a few bells going off. If so, you will need to evaluate those areas very carefully. How

HOW DO FREELANCERS COMPENSATE FOR LACK OF BENEFITS?

Freelancers charge their clients a higher hourly rate for their services than a salaried employee receives because they must compensate themselves for their time as well as for the cost of operating their businesses. Operating costs include rent, utilities, supplies, equipment, and health insurance.

If you intend to freelance, here is an easy-to-follow formula for determining your hourly rates:

1. First figure out what you want to be paid as a fair hourly fee for your services.

2. Then add in your operating costs:

   • Add up your projected yearly operating expenses and divide that figure by 12 months

   • Divide that figure by 4 weeks per month to get a monthly rate

   • Divide that amount by 5 days a week to get a weekly rate

   • Then divide that figure by 8 hours a day to get an hourly rate.

3. Add the final amount from step 2 to your service fee in step 1 and that amount is your hourly freelance rate.

As your operating expenses increase and your experience makes your services more valuable you can raise your rates accordingly.

---

do you really feel about the things you will have to do in this job? How much time away from your family or your personal life will this job consume? Can you live comfortably with that? Was there any indication that you might be asked to do something that you would find personally uncomfortable?

Take a close look at Step One, Workshop 5: Deciding When to Compromise—Values versus Confidence. If you sense that you will be required to do something that you have listed in this exercise as a definite "no compromise" issue, then you may want to go back and speak candidly to your interviewer about your concerns. If this issue is a value, not a fear, and the interviewer will not budge on your involvement in this area, then you may have to be prepared to walk away. If you do, remember that true success is not what job you have or how much money you make, but how happy you are with what you are doing. If you allow yourself to be compromised on an issue that is important to any facet of your life, you will not be happy in this job for long.

If you are offered the wrong job

If you do discover that a nagging feeling keeps haunting you—telling you that this is not the job for you, then you need to honor that feeling. The wrong job will never turn into the right job. And you will never be happy in the wrong job.

If all attempts to reach a negotiable compromise with your would-be employer have failed, then you have reached a crossroads. You must walk away and trust that the right job is waiting for you. I like to think of every situation like this as a test to see just how important the right conditions are to me when an opportunity presents itself. If I can remain true to my values and integrity and walk away, I have always been rewarded with a far better opportunity that was just around the next corner. It took awhile for me to trust that this would happen. But it has not failed me yet.

The rejection

What if you do get that rejection letter? What do you do then? Nothing? Walk away and forget that you ever heard of that agency? Well, you could do that. But how would that help you when it comes time to go to your next interview?

If you did not get the job, it could have been that someone else more qualified, more intelligent, or more attractive came along. But the real truth could be that the person the agency hired was no more qualified, no more intelligent, and no more attractive than you. It could be that you answered a question or two in a way that gave your interviewer the wrong impression of you. Or you may have lacked certain kinds of work in your portfolio. Or maybe you forgot to tell your interviewer an important piece of information about yourself that could have turned the tide in your favor. If you did something that you could have avoided or corrected or made clearer, do you want to take a chance that you will do that same thing during your next interview?

Every rejection and every failure that you experience in your life is nothing more than an opportunity to find out what you could have done better. If you learn from that experience and apply it to the next situation, it will put you another step closer to success.

Call your interviewer and explain that you want to learn from this experience and would like to know why you were not chosen for the position. An honest answer will help you overcome any weaknesses in your interviewing skills. If you find out that the decision not to hire you was based on a lack of certain experience or training, knowing what areas to focus your efforts on in the future could be extremely valuable.

Careers in Advertising—your options to agency employment

What if, after all this, you are beginning to get the idea that you love advertising but you hate the thought of working in an advertising agency? Maybe you sense that the pressure might be too much when you have other responsibilities in your life. Whatever it is that is setting off warning signals for you, listen to them, honor them.

You do have other options. You can still work in advertising creating campaigns, designing brochures and ads, developing radio and TV commercials, all the fun and exciting stuff, without the pressure that can be an ever-present reality in the agency business. Some people thrive under that pressure. It can send their spirits soaring. But if your spirits fall into the pits of hopelessness when pressure comes your way, take heart: there are choices galore.

Design Studios

Your first option is a design studio. Design studios are usually small, one- or two-person shops that specialize only in graphics or designing specialty items. They do not get involved, usually, in major ad campaigns or buying media. As a result the work pace is considerably more manageable on a day-to-day basis. Although design studios still face project deadlines, the atmosphere is generally a little less frenzied than a typical ad agency.

Publishing Companies

Publishing companies offer great opportunities for either creative types or the business/management crowd. Publishing companies produce printed materials that range from newspapers, tabloids, and circulars to magazines and books.

It would be misleading to say that publishing is not a pressured business. It is. When a publication is approaching press time, all hell can break loose. But the saving grace is that you are only working for *one* boss—the company. In an advertising agency you are always working for the client—and there are *many* of them, pulling multiple strings at once. Agency owners are always dancing to the tunes their clients play, and you will be expected to dance along as well.

Print Houses

Working for a printer can be hectic and fast paced, but the customers, even though they may be demanding, will still have to acquiesce to the printer's schedule.

Print houses, large and small, hire many artists. But the work they do is usually restricted to mechanical preparation, generating computer type, and occasionally designing something or doing some illustration. So if you want to do quality design or illustration work, you are better off looking toward the other options mentioned here. Printers almost never hire a copywriter or photographer.

Corporate, In-house Advertising Departments

If the thought of dealing with clients and all their demands gives you the willies, you can always go over to the other side. You can become the client!

A corporation includes just about any type of company from high-tech industrial corporations and Fortune 500 companies to manufacturing companies, retail chains, and banks. If you work in an in-house advertising department of one of these corporations, you will not only develop and produce company-related promotional materials, you will most likely be involved in working with that company's ad agency. That will make you the client. What fun! Now you can be the one who gets to be around all those creative geniuses, feel the excitement as you work with them to come up with great ideas for your company, but let them worry about the deadlines and pleasing you.

In a corporate environment you will still have deadlines to face, corporate grapevines to dodge, and conservative management to worry about. But again you will only work for one boss—the company. That, plus the somewhat more secure feeling that you will not lose your job the instant business drops off or a major client is lost, can help you sleep a little better at night.

Nonprofit Corporations

If you enjoy a corporate type of environment, the security of an institution, an even slower, more predictable pace, and you still like the idea of being the client, try looking into nonprofit organizations or institutions. There are many groups that fall into the nonprofit category. Just look in the Yellow Pages under either heading and you will see plenty to choose from. I am talking about organizations like the Red Cross, the United Way, Volunteers in Action, the American Lung Association, and on and on. Many institutions are also nonprofit corporations, such as schools, colleges and universities, hospitals, medical centers, the military, local, state, and federal government agencies, credit unions, etc.

Nonprofits have in-house advertising departments, marketing or publications departments, or public relations offices which hire graphic designers, copywriters, marketing, and research people. They get involved in just about everything that ad agencies do, including media buying. If you go to work for a nonprofit, you will also, in most cases, have the opportunity to work directly with ad agencies, since most institutions hire agencies to handle their major promotions or campaigns.

The main advantage of working for a nonprofit corporation is that once you get hired and do a relatively good job, your position will be far more secure than any of the other options presented here. Since nonprofit organizations or institutions do not have to show a profit, they are less subject to a slumping economy. But they are not immune. The one thing you will have to watch out for is budget cuts on a state or federal level if your nonprofit company or agency is heavily funded by governmental sources.

The pay scale may be far less attractive in a nonprofit, but the short- and long-term benefits, such as health insurance, tuition reimbursement, and retirement pensions, will usually outweigh the up-front cash incentive.

Keep the job once you get it

Join the agency

You got it! Your first job in advertising. The salary is more than you expected. The benefits are adequate. You will even have your own office. And the position, as described by your new boss, seems exactly what you wanted. What more could you ask for? All that work researching those agencies, doing all those exercises in this book, writing your cover letters, the resume, preparing for interviews, the tension, the worry—well, it is all over now. Now you can kick your feet up, take a deep breath, and enjoy the ride into your future in advertising.

Enjoy the ride? Absolutely! Kick your feet up and relax? Not a chance! Getting the job is only half the battle. The other half is keeping it.

How do you keep a job? Get to work on time and do your best each day? That is a start. But it is only a small part of what is involved in keeping a job—especially a job in advertising. Some people believe that the only way to survive in advertising is to be smarter and more creative than anyone else in the agency. These same people believe that you are only as good as your last good idea. They spend all their time thinking about how to look good in the eyes of their employer. There are plenty of people just like this in advertising agencies all over the world. And you will definitely run into more than your share. But whatever you do, if you want to stay in advertising, do not become one of them.

Egoitis—a deadly disease

The last thing an agency owner wants to deal with is competitiveness within the agency. There is enough of that going on between agencies. As soon as one person becomes more concerned about personal performance in the agency and how that performance is being evaluated by agency management, that person is no longer thinking about the good of the agency. That person is thinking only about self. I call this *egoitis*. And egoitis kills more people in advertising than all the stress, the pressure, and rapid pace combined. People who suffer from egoitis do not leave advertising burnt out and exhausted because they put such demanding expectations on themselves to be the best. They usually leave because they have been fired.

You may be thinking, what is wrong with trying to be the most creative person in the agency? To be the best or the most creative designer or copywriter or anything else requires a person to constantly make comparisons with someone else. When a comparison is drawn between one person and others, one is the winner and the remaining people are the losers, by virtue of the fact that they are just not as good as the person who is the best or the most. That kind of situation creates rivalry, resentment, and a complete breakdown in the ability of agency employees to trust and share ideas and thoughts with each other. If you are working with someone who is more concerned about showing the boss what a creative genius he is, are you going to be willing to tell him about your terrific idea for an ad campaign for the agency's new account? No, of course not! He might try to pass it off as his own.

Great ideas in an ad agency need to be explored and expanded upon so that all aspects of the campaign can be adapted to them. That takes team input and brainstorming along with an objectivity that can only be maintained when no one in the group is attached to ownership of the idea. Objectivity is essential, because if the idea does not develop into an ad that will produce results for the client, then the idea, as creative as it may be, is worthless.

Advertising is a team sport

Every ad agency is run like a sports team. One player cannot win the game all alone. No matter how great that player may be, nothing can be accomplished without the support and cooperation of the other team members.

In an agency, the goal of the game is to win the approval and devotion of the client. In other words, the client approves if he likes what the agency is doing for him. And he shows his devotion by giving the agency another project or campaign to work on. The only way to win the approval and devotion of the client is to give the client what he wants—a successful ad campaign. What is a successful ad campaign? One that sells the client's product or service. If one egotistical designer or copywriter is focused entirely on how clever she has been in coming up with a new ad, she may mistake cleverness for effectiveness.

This happens a lot. People think that creativity—which means to create something new that never existed in exactly this form before—will automatically grab the viewer's attention. It may, simply because people tend to look at something they have never seen before. But that does not mean it will make them want it, recognize it, or ever think about it again. And if an ad catches people's attention but does not make them want to buy what the ad is selling, the client is not going to be happy. So the designer or copywriter who ignores the opinions and judgments of the rest of the creative team in lieu of her own clever ideas may win an award at the next ad show but drive the client away from the agency. Without clients there is no agency. Always keep that foremost in your mind.

To keep your job, you have to help your agency win and keep the approval of each and every client. That means becoming a team player whose focus is on pleasing the client by creating ads, brochures, or any other kinds of promotional materials that sell. To quote the statement that we put on the front of our agency brochure: "Creativity is one thing . . . results are something else." And your agency, too, will be working toward one objective: results. That will always come before any one person's great idea.

Understand how the business works

To be an effective team player, you have to know how the game is played. That means understanding game strategies and how they work. Most important of all, is knowing what the goal is. The goal is keeping the client happy. The game strategies include:

- How an agency is structured
- How an agency makes money
- How an agency gets clients and keeps clients
- How an agency builds its reputation

The remainder of this chapter will give the information you will need about the business of advertising and the strategies necessary to play the game well.

Agency priorities

Advertising agencies are concerned about only one thing: staying in business. To stay in business, an agency must have clients, service those clients, bill the clients for those services, make enough money from the clients to pay the agency's bills (rent, utilities, salaries, and other operating expenses), and then hopefully earn a profit when all the bills have been paid.

Agency owners discover that in order to succeed in business, they must develop a set of priorities that determines what is important to the agency. Those priorities, which tend to be the same for almost every agency owner, are as follows:

1. Putting the client—always, without exception—first
2. Making a profit
3. Producing quality work
4. Developing creative, fresh, and innovative approaches to projects and campaigns
5. Having a reputation for fair and ethical business practices
6. Satisfying management with jobs, salaries, and benefits
7. Satisfying employees with jobs, salaries, and benefits—always a last priority

Every wise employee will take note of this list of priorities. If you ever find yourself thinking that the agency does not care about how creative you are being and is willing to sacrifice your ideas for a stuffy old client's stale ideas, you are absolutely right. And threatening to quit will do you absolutely no good. As you can see by this list of priorities, clients will always come before creativity, and your happiness on the job is the lowest rung on the ladder. Do not think it will be any different at another agency. If an agency is going to stay in business, the priorities the agency management sets has to follow the same list.

How an agency gets clients

To have clients an agency has to get them. That becomes the responsibility of the account executive or A.E. An A.E. is the agency's salesperson first and account manager second. The A.E. brings new business (clients) into the agency in several ways:

- Cold Calls
  This involves picking up the phone and calling area businesses to see if they are presently working with an agency. If not, then the A.E. will request an opportunity to come in and meet with the owner to explain how an ad agency can help the business to grow.

- Networking
  The A.E. will join business clubs and organizations to meet owners of local businesses and executives from the corporate and nonprofit sectors who may be looking for an ad agency or know of people who are.

- Referrals
  Clients and vendors who do business with ad agencies will often recommend the agency to others. After an agency has been in business for a while, this can become a major source of new business.

Once an account executive finds a potential lead for a new account, the next step is to try to set up an appointment with the business owner or company representative. During the first meeting, the A.E. will assess whether or not this account is worth pursuing. That decision is based on the amount of money that the company is willing to spend on its advertising for the year and if the owner or company representative appears sincerely interested in working with the agency.

If a company's budget for advertising is very low, it may not be possible for the agency to make any money on that account. Some agencies will only accept an account if the yearly budget meets a minimum amount. That is usually determined by the size of the agency and the prices it charges. For some smaller agencies, that minimum might be as low as ten or twenty thousand dollars a year, and for larger agencies it might have to be at least one hundred thousand dollars or more a year. There are some agencies who will take work from a business or company on a project-by-project basis and will not be concerned with how much revenue will be generated for the year.

Presentations

With lower-budget accounts or projects, the A.E. can often convince the owner or company representative to give the agency a try just after one or two meetings. For an account that represents not only more money but also the possibility of other competitive agencies knocking on this company's door, the A.E. may have to offer the company a presentation. A presentation is a formal meeting between the A.E. and several other agency people—called the account team—and several key people from the company—usually upper management and company officers.

During this meeting the agency will present a proposal that will outline exactly what the agency intends to do to promote the company's product or service. (From here on I will refer to the company's product or service as the "product" for the sake of simplicity.) That proposal will also include how much the company will have to spend to pay the agency to do this and how much the advertising itself will cost, such as radio, TV, newspapers, brochures, etc. The agency account team will then show samples of the creative ideas the agency has come up with, such as ad designs, copy for the ads, and if television commercials are involved, samples of commercial storyboards, and so on. The company may also be reviewing presentations from other agencies as well and then comparing each agency for price, services capabilities, whether or not the agency's ideas will work, and if they believe that the agency can accomplish what it promises.

The agency account team prepares for a presentation by going through three steps.

Research   The account team researches the company's history, the competition, and the current and future trends of the company's product in the marketplace.

Positioning   By looking at the information gathered during the research phase, the account team can then decide how to position the client's product, first in relation to the competition the product has in the marketplace, and second in terms of how to get the target audience interested in purchasing it.

Strategy   Based on how the agency intends to position the product, the account team then develops a strategy plan that details exactly how the product will be presented (the advertising concept) to the target audience, the media mix that will be used (radio, television, newspapers, billboards, etc.), and the frequency in which the ads will appear (i.e., how many times a day an ad will run on a particular TV station and for how many weeks).

Elements of an ad campaign

With these three steps completed, the agency account team now has all the information it needs to put together an entire campaign. There are eight components we will look at.

1. Creative concepts   This is the approach that will be used in the ads, brochures, etc., to get the message noticed and then acted upon by the target audience.

2. Designs, slogans, and copy   When the creative concept have been agreed to, then the art and copy departments can begin to work on the various designs, the slogans, and the copy that will be used based on those concepts.

3. Media plan and costs   Now that the strategy has been decided upon, the media people can put together a media plan (where and when the ads will run) for the campaign. From that they can figure out the client's cost to advertise the product.

4. Cost for creative and production services   The art director now has an understanding of what will be needed to put the entire campaign together from the art department's perspective. That means exactly how many ads will need to be designed and if brochures or other collateral printed pieces are to be developed, what that will involve and how much time it will take the art department to produce them. And what materials will be used in the production of the artwork for the ads and collateral pieces. With this information the art director can figure out how much creative and production services will cost the client based on time and materials. (The use of the word materials here is meant to mean not only art department supplies such as boards and markers, but also includes typesetting, printing, and stat costs, as well as figuring in the cost for hiring outside people to do photography or illustration if the campaign requires it.)

5. Cost for copy services   The head of the copy department now knows how much copy will be needed and how much time that will take the department to complete it. Based on that, the cost to produce the copy can be estimated.

6. Cost to service the account   Once the A.E. knows exactly what the campaign will entail, the hours spent servicing the account can be approximated and the cost to the client can be estimated. Servicing an account involves meeting with the client whenever necessary, supervising art and copy production, print production, radio and television production, and billing.

7. Total cost for the campaign   All the estimated costs would be given to the agency's financial manager, and a complete cost projection estimate would be prepared for the client.

8. Project schedule   The agency's production manager would confer with the art director, the copy director, the creative director, the A.E., the media buyer and planner assigned to the account, and the traffic coordinator to put together a production schedule for the campaign. A production schedule breaks the campaign down into stages of development and indicates when each stage is due and who is involved.

When all eight elements of the campaign preparation are completed, the agency account team would then review them with agency's management. Once they gave the concept, the designs, the media plans and schedules, cost projections, and production schedule their approval, the account team would be ready to show all of this to the client in a presentation.

Building flexibility and choices into the campaign presentation

During the presentation the client has an opportunity to give the account team some feedback on the campaign elements. If the client does not like the concept, then that can throw a major upset into the whole campaign plan. Revising the concept is one thing, but coming up with a totally new concept will mean that the ad designs and copy prepared thus far will have to be scrapped. It is for this reason alone that the creative people working on a campaign usually come up with several concepts to present to a client and several different designs and copy samples to go along with the various concepts. The designs themselves are generally done in a sketch or idea format. This is, they are not completely polished and finished, since it is extremely rare that a client will accept what an agency presents without changes.

How to prepare and give a presentation

While it probably will not happen until you have been working in an agency for at least a year, eventually you may be asked to participate in the actual delivery of a presentation. Do not let this panic you. Presentations can be a little scary at first, but just like the apprehension you had when it came to your first agency interview, the other interviews became much easier after that. You can take comfort in knowing that presentations are always given by an agency team, so you will not be doing it alone. It is so much easier and even fun to go in excited by the spirit of the work you have created together, and face a client or even a committee of people as a unified and well-rehearsed group, and give them your best. In fact, presentations can be a real high in agency work.

You and your team will work very hard for a period of three or four weeks to produce a campaign that is both creative and based on sound research and advertising know-how. Then, when you go in and present what you believe is your best work, you get an immediate response—which is usually excitement, enthusiasm, and appreciation for your talent and expertise. Even if your agency is not hired, you will rarely experience a negative reaction from a potential client during a presentation. Clients may prefer another agency's approach or prices, but they still get impressed with the quality of the work.

Presentations are one of the most important aspects of agency business because this is how most accounts, especially large budget accounts, are won. But presentations are also very hard on an agency because they require that agency people who are already working to full capacity on present accounts find extra time and energy to do the work of developing a whole new campaign. And all this has to be done without the guarantee that the agency will even get the account. Furthermore, an agency cannot bill a client for the work put into a presentation unless the account is won. And yet, the agency still has to pay its people who are spending agency hours on a potentially unbillable project.

But there is an up side to presentations, even if they result in not winning the account. The work and ideas that go into a presentation are never wasted. You will almost always find that there is another client your agency already has, or possibly a new one that is coming right around the corner, whose account would be perfect for these same concepts and creative ideas. It always seems to work out that way.

PRESENTATION DO'S AND DON'TS

Because presentations are so important to an agency, not to mention expensive, I have put together a list of presentation do's and don'ts. A run through this list will help you stay focused on your responsibility in a presentation, regardless of your position in the agency. It will also help you avoid any first time mistakes or misconceptions if you do become part of a presentation team.

1. Presentations should be taken very seriously by every member of the account team. Every effort should be made to give a presentation the same preparation, thought, and creativity that a paying client would receive.

2. Presentations should be well-prepared and rehearsed many times by the entire presentation account team to be certain that there are no awkward pauses. The presentation team will need to determine ahead of time what questions might be asked and exactly how they will be answered.

3. Presentations should always be slanted toward the point of view of the client.

4. Always make sure there is no part of the presentation that cannot be substantiated by research information or is not based on sound knowledge and experience.

5. Presentations are often called "dog and pony shows" because that is exactly what they are—a performance. As such, they should be timed, fast moving, informative, and entertaining without being silly or trivial.

6. As a member of a presentation team, your participation and preparation is critical. Never let your team members down. There is nothing more awkward than a member of a presentation team who is not well prepared for the presentation.

The written proposal

The written presentation proposal will contain everything you will say during the actual presentation. So what is the reason for having a written proposal? The answer is simple: it is something that you can leave behind for the client and the committee members to look through after other competitive agencies make their presentations. By comparing your agency's proposal and those left by other agencies, the committee can see clearly where there are similarities and differences, and what they like and do not like. Memories of an agency's presentation will fade quickly when a committee has to sit through several presentations. All the agencies begin to look and sound alike. A written proposal will continue speaking for your agency long after the presentation is over.

7. The written proposal part of the presentation should be distributed to the client and presentation committee members. The proposal copies should be inserted or bound in a presentation folder—most agencies have their own. It is a nice touch to individualize copies of the proposal by having each committee member's name on that person's personal copy. This can be done with a computer or with individualized labels on the dover of the presentation folders.

8. Agency presenters should never read from their presentation packet. It looks unprofessional. Notes are acceptable as an occasional reference only.

9. All artwork should be enlarged and mounted on boards, with cover paper attached to the boards. Keep the work covered until you or a member of your presentation team is ready to talk about the work. This way the client cannot look at it out of context.

10. Charts, graphs, and any other relevant materials such as storyboards, slides, videos, or audio tapes should only be shown or played at the precise point in which they are being referred to in the presentation.

11. If the presentation is at the agency, then light refreshments add a nice touch. Never serve alcohol.

12. The appropriate dress for presentations is determined by the client and the nature of the presentation. If it is a formal presentation in a conference room with a number of people from the client's company, then you should wear a suit. If you are meeting informally with just the client and maybe a few other people in the client's office, then a sports jacket and tie or even an open shirt may be acceptable, especially if the client is more on the informal side. You do not want to overdress if the client tends to wear chinos or jeans. On the other hand, you do not want to dress down too much, either.

The written proposal should contain the following information:

- Statement of purpose
An opening statement explaining the reason for the presentation

- Definition of the target audience
Identifying specifically who the audience—buyers and users—of the client's product or service will be

- Demographics
A breakdown of the various characteristics that make up the target audience, i.e., age, gender, economic brackets, race, color, creed, and taste preferences based on current market data

- Goals
Exactly what the agency intends to accomplish for the client's company

- Market research report
An outline of the market research the agency has compiled

- Campaign strategy
How the agency will achieve its intended goals, based on the positioning concept, the creative concept, and the planned media mix

- Proposed budget
An itemized breakdown of all projected expenditures the client will be responsible for in the campaign, including media costs, agency fees not defrayed by media commissions, production costs (typesetting, printing, photography, stats, special expenses such as slides, computer-generated materials, illustrations, etc.), clerical, mailing, fax, and other miscellaneous expenses

- Media schedule (if applicable)
A listing of all media to be used, and the date, time, and frequency of each ad's appearance

- Copies of all related artwork, copy, scripts, and storyboards
When the written proposal is distributed to the committee members before the presentation begins, it is a good idea to ask them to refrain from reading it during the presentation. If the committee members are allowed to flip through the proposal while your team is delivering their verbal presentation, chances are that many of them will not be listening. Furthermore, they will be reading ahead, knowing exactly what you or someone else on your team is going to say next. That will take the impact out of your delivery.

The only time you may want to instruct them to look at the proposal is when it comes time to explain the budget breakdown or the media schedule or some other information that is complex and requires facts and figures to back up what your team is saying. At that point you can direct them to the exact page the information is located on, go through it, and then ask them to put the proposal aside again.

Working on the actual campaign

If the client decides to award the agency the account, the actual work on the campaign can begin. The work itself can be divided into three distinct stages—development of concept, production of concept, and implementation of the campaign. Each of these stages is presented below, along with the progressive steps that must be taken to complete each stage. It is important that you become completely familiar with these stages because they are the foundation of the work you will do in an agency.

Stage 1: Development of concept

1. Positioning, research, and strategy
2. Creative concepts
3. Preliminary design sketches and copy
4. Media plans and budget
5. Client approval of all preliminary work

Stage 2: Production of concept

1. Client's requested revisions incorporated into the concept
2. Finalized designs, copy, scripts, and storyboards produced
3. Photographs taken, if necessary
4. Client approval of finished designs, copy, storyboards, and scripts
5. Mechanicals of all ads and printed materials produced
6. Client approval of mechanicals for printed materials
7. Mechanicals delivered to printer
8. Radio and TV commercials produced

Stage 3: Implementation of campaign

1. Completed commercials distributed to appropriate stations, and completed print ads sent out to newspapers and magazines
2. Printed collateral pieces delivered from printer and mailed or distributed
3. Commercials begin airing, and print ads start their publication runs

That completes the entire development and implementation of an advertising campaign. At this point, the client can be billed for all media scheduled to run and all other related campaign expenses and agency fees.

Working with clients

Clients are the most important part of an advertising agency. They are the business. Without clients an agency cannot stay in business. Agency employees, particularly those in the creative departments such as copy and design, and new employees often lose sight of the client's position within the structure of the agency. Creative people can sometimes get so caught up in the "art" of their work that they focus more on that than on pleasing the client. And the new employee is usually just totally unaware of the importance of the client to the agency.

Agency owners do care about the quality of the work produced by their agency, but if the work itself does not meet the goals promised the client, like increasing visibility or sales, the client may look for another agency. And that can make agency owners nervous. Agency owners also get nervous at the thought of losing a client because someone at the agency made a mistake or said something that angered the client. Even though it is an accepted fact that clients come and go and an agency cannot keep a client indefinitely, even when it is doing a great job, agency owners still put all of their energy into pleasing their clients and making sure their employees do, too. But clients tend to get restless regardless of the effort an agency makes on their behalf. They always tend to wonder if maybe another agency could do a better job. Plus, clients are constantly courted by other agencies who want their business. And they are being offered irresistible prices and guarantees if they will leave their present agency and switch. But when a client fires an agency because the agency made an unforgivable error, that is not only a slap in the face to an agency, but it is also a nasty blow to the agency's reputation.

If you can possibly avoid it, you do not ever want to be the one person at the agency who caused irreparable damage with a client through ignorance or a careless oversight. To prevent that from happening, you need to be armed with all the information you can get about how to work well with clients. That means understanding what clients need, want, and expect in a relationship with their agency and its employees. Also, you must have a thorough understanding of your agency's procedures for handling projects. This will help you catch problems before they begin.

Building good client relationships

It takes two things to build a good relationship with clients:

- Always try to see things from the client's perspective.
- Be responsive and attentive to the client's needs.

Incidentally, this is also the key to building a good relationship with your employer.

Clients pay an agency a lot of money for only one reason—to increase their business. The agency does this by developing a plan that will get whatever it is that the client's company sells noticed by the people who will buy it. It is that simple. And if your agency does not accomplish that goal, your agency is not meeting your client's needs.

Beyond that, a good relationship with a client is built on respect for the client's opinions and expertise in the work the client's company produces. I know of some agencies who totally disrespect their clients and do not bother to hide it. They deal with their clients from a position of superiority. The management and even employees at these agencies act as though they are the only authorities who know how to market and advertise a product. They are condescending in their attitude toward their clients and bully them into going along with their agency's creative ideas, even when the client protests that it will not work.

I know about these agencies, because a number of their clients came to my agency when they were finally fed up with the treatment they had been receiving. In addition, most of these runaway clients told me that not only were the people at their former agencies ill-mannered, but for all their boasting about how creative and knowledgeable they were, their work had failed to deliver results.

Most clients do know their business, or they would not be in it. They know who their market is and what motivates these people to buy their product. And they know the strengths and weaknesses of their product. It is up to you to listen to what your clients tell you, believe them, and learn everything you can from them about their company, their product, and their market.

Occasionally you will run into clients who really do not know anything, or clients who know a lot but do not know how to apply that to a workable advertising program. When you happen across one of these types, you will need to do some extra homework and find out what you need to know to help them position and advertise their product. But the most important thing to remember is never tell clients that they know nothing. If you need to convince a client that a particular idea your agency has developed is better than the client's idea, do it with tact and respect. Something that works well with clients is to do what they want but also show them an example of what the agency wants to do. Then let them do their own side-by-side comparison. It is the rare client who will see their bad idea alongside the agency's great concept and not be able to tell which one is more effective.

If all attempts fail, and your client still insists on having the agency produce the client's idea, that is when you have to step aside and let your agency owners decide what to do. You can tell the client that you will inform your supervisor or the agency president or whoever would be involved in the account what the client has decided. If the agency is willing to risk losing the client before it will do poor quality work, it is their decision to make. You do not ever want to say to a client that your agency will not get involved in producing second rate advertising on the assumption that they will applaud you for upholding their integrity but losing a client. At all costs, keep yourself out of compromising situations. Speak only for your agency when you are authorized to do so. Always defer final judgment on any issue, including cost, to agency higher-ups.

Speaking of cost, another responsibility that an agency has to a client is to deliver the work promised at the cost the agency and client have agreed to. If you are in a position in which the work you do in any way effects the cost a client will have to pay for a project, make sure you know to the penny what the agency has quoted the client, and then make sure that whatever you do does not increase that cost.

I once had an art director who was given the responsibility of putting together price quotes for client projects. This fellow was a very talented designer with exquisite taste. As a result, it was his desire that every design that he produced or that he supervised being produced be done with only the best quality materials. That meant that when he went out to bid for a print job, he would get price quotes based on the most expensive paper, PMS ink colors when a house ink would have done the job just as well, etc.

It is not that I prefer cutting corners; I do not. I, too, want to produce the highest quality work that the client's budget will allow. But the important consideration here is what the client can afford. If a client only has a $5,000 budget for design and printing of his brochures, and the agency has agreed to work within that budget, then you cannot turn around and surprise the client with a bill that is $1,500 more because you thought a certain kind of paper was more fashionable.

The worse part about what this art director did was that he concealed the real cost for quite a few print jobs for a period of several months. He did it by adjusting his price quote from a printer if it was beyond the limits of the client's budget, and making it conform to what the client had to spend. Then a month or so after the client's project was finished, the bill from the printer would come in. When it did, he would intercept it and bury it in with other bills so that my bookkeeper would not catch the discrepancy between the invoice price and the amount billed to the client. This went on until one day my accountant noticed the imbalance between money paid out to printers and money billed to clients for printing. When we began to investigate, we discovered that the cover-up was not just limited to printing quotes; it also included reprographic services and typesetting fees.

My art director's taste preferences turned out to cost my agency over $3,000 in cost overruns that could not be recouped. And the hardest thing for me to understand was that it was deliberate on his part. He operated on the assumption that bills came in and no one double-checked them for validity against the original quote. He was right, for a while. My bookkeeper was busy and often overworked and had let quite a few bills slide by without cross referencing. She was mortified to discover her mistake and assured me that she had learned a very important lesson and would from here on never let a bill go unconfirmed. The art director was not as accepting of his error. He maintained that clients were stupid, and even if it cost the agency more money, we should be willing to pay the difference for whatever it cost to produce the highest quality work. I asked if he was willing to give up a percentage of his salary to contribute to that cause. That was a different story. He was not willing to do that. As you may have surmised, that moment was his last with my agency.

Mistakes can happen. But when they do, never try to cover them up. When they are discovered, and inevitably they will be discovered by someone, it will be far more dangerous for you. The wisest thing you can do in the face of any kind of mistake is to go directly to the agency owner and tell exactly what happened. I advise you not to go to your supervisor because that puts that person in the middle of the situation. In addition, your supervisor may insist on trying to correct it and only succeed in making it worse. Or if your supervisor decides to tell the agency owner what happened for you, the owner will not have the benefit of hearing directly from you how sorry you are, or why or how it happened, and your sincere intentions to correct the mistake or pay for it if necessary.

It is rare that an agency owner would insist that an employee pay for a financial blunder that cost the agency money. I certainly would not have wanted my art director to make up the $3,000 loss. Just having him accept responsibility, admit that it was an error in judgement, and assure me that it would not happen again was all I needed. After all, he was an excellent designer. But his personal standards became more important than respecting the agency's position or the client's budget.

Client meetings

Client meetings can be the beginning or the end of a good and mutually beneficial agency/client relationship. Meetings, whether in person or scheduled telephone meetings, are the forum in which the agency and client communicate. Using this forum to lay the groundwork for an open and honest relationship should be the number one concern of anyone who is working with a client. If that person is you, there are some basic practices that you can use that will help you establish long-lasting associations with your clients. They are as follows:

1. Be considerate of your client's time. Always schedule a meeting at the client's convenience and in the location of the client's choice.

2. Go into the first and every other client meeting prepared to listen very carefully to your client.

3. Find out as much as you can about the client's company, the market, the company's goals and expectations.

    To get this information, it is sometimes necessary to prompt the client. Many of them don't know what to say or what to tell you. It may be hard for them to decide what is important and what is not.

4. Go to each meeting with a well-prepared list of open-ended questions about the client's project, the goals of the project, the specifications, the budget, or any other detailed information that you need to know.

    Questions will encourage your client to open up and tell you exactly what you need to know to help your agency do its job, which is to meet the client's needs.

5. If you are meeting with a client for the first time, do not try to sell that client on your agency's capabilities.

    Find out instead what you or your agency can do to help the client. Clients are more interested in themselves and their needs than the agency's past track record and list of successful achievements.

6. To be sure that you have clearly understood your client, take a few minutes during the last part of the meeting to reflect back to the client what you think has been said or asked for.

   That way, if you have misunderstood anything or there were any mistaken impressions on the client's part, you will both have the opportunity to clear it up right then and there, before it turns into a problem.

7. If you have rescheduled a client meeting (for whatever reason) always do it in a professional way.

   Keep your personal life and personal reasons out of the explanation about why you have to cancel the meeting. Clients do not want to hear that you have to take your son to the dentist or get home early to make dinner. That is your problem, not theirs. And it is best not to offer a detailed excuse when you do cancel. You can simply say that something important has come up at the office, and would it be possible to reschedule? While it may be a lie to say that something has come up at the office, it is always more professional to cancel a meeting because of a professional problem rather than a personal problem. Unless the personal problem is life-threatening to you or someone else, mixing your private life with work-related issues can give the client the impression that your personal life comes before your work. And the fact is that may be true, but you want to do your best not to let clients know that.

8. Never, never keep a client waiting.

   If you are going to be late always call ahead and ask if the delay will inconvenience your client. If it will, then find another time that will better suit the client's schedule.

9. Always dress appropriately for client meetings.

   Even if you work in the art department where everyone dresses more casually than management or the account executives, if you have to meet with a client, dress for the client.

10. If you make a mistake with some aspect of a client's project, be honest and up-front about it as soon as possible.

    Do not wait to get caught to admit that something you have done has gone wrong. Your client will appreciate you candor.

Working with vendors and subcontractors

Next to clients, vendors are the second most important people agency employees will come into contact with. No agency can produce all their own work in-house, so vendors and subcontractors are essential when it comes to completing agency projects.

A vendor is someone or some company that sells a product or service to another company. A subcontractor sells his or her talent in the form of a service. The word talent is the main difference between a vendor and subcontractor. A printing company, art supplier, paper company, color separator, reprographic specialist (people who make stats, films, and negatives) are usually called vendors. Photographers, videographers, voice and acting talent, illustrators, and other freelance people such as copywriters and paste-up artists are hired on a subcontracting basis to produce or complete a specific part of a project that cannot be done by the agency's own staff. The reason it cannot be done by the agency might be because no one in the agency has the particular talent necessary to do the job or the staff is too backed up with work and needs to farm out a part of the project.

Good vendor relationships are extremely important to an agency for a variety of reasons. When you have to meet a deadline, and you need a printer or type-setter or photographer who is willing to work overtime or squeeze your job in at the last minute, you had better be on good terms with that person. People in business will go out of their way to help out each other, because we all know our turn will come. If you treat vendors and subcontractors as if they are your servants, they will not be there for you when the chips are down.

It is very important to be fair in your dealings with vendors and subcontractors. Do not blame them when something goes wrong, just to get off the hook with your boss or client. Be as honest with them about your mistakes and your shortcomings as you would with a colleague. And give them all the information they need to do their best job, which includes giving them plenty of lead time on deadlines. Keep them informed when a deadline is approaching. Do not assume that they are as aware of every detail of your project as you are. Put all their directions and specifications for a job in writing. Compliment them when they do a good or great job. When you receive a client's praise for a project, pass it on to everyone else involved in the project. Direct business referrals to them whenever you can, and they will do the same for you.

Vendors and subcontractors will become the messengers of your agency's good or bad reputation. News in the advertising community travels fastest. So always be very careful what you say about your agency or a client to one of your vendors or subcontractors. Bad vendor/subcontractor relationships can break an agency. These people have important contacts throughout the advertising community, not only with other vendors and subcontractors, but with your agency's clients and potential new clients as well. They can be an agency's greatest source of new business referrals or the greatest source for discouraging new business from even considering your agency.

Pricing and budget

It is not just art directors who are responsible for putting together price quotes and making sure a project stays within a client's budget. Project managers, media buyers, financial managers, account coordinators, assistants, and secretaries, too, are all involved in soliciting bids from vendors, subcontractors, and media sales-people and compiling that information into a price quote or estimate. And these same people are responsible for maintaining the cost–accounting records on projects for billing purposes. Whatever position you are hired for, chances are that one day your turn will come, too, and you will find yourself trying to get some prices and write up a quote. When that happens, you want to be prepared with the "how to's" of putting a bid together, soliciting bids, and adding in markup. So here goes, a whirlwind introduction to budget breakdowns, pricing a job, and cost control.

Breaking down the budget

Budgets represent the amount of money a client sets aside for a single project or an entire campaign. Whether that amount is $500 or $500,000, it is up to the agency to first decide if what the client wants to do can be accomplished with that amount of money. The only way to know is to take the total amount of the budget and break it down into all the components of the project.

For example, suppose a client has $5,500 to spend on a capabilities brochure. She asks you if you can do this project for that amount of money. You say, "Well, let's put together the specs." That means all the specifications or details of the project. To do that, you have to ask the client questions. To begin with you ask, "How many brochures do you need?" She says, "5,000." Then you ask her how much information she want to have in the brochure. She hands you several pages of copy. "What about visuals, do you want photographs or illustrations?" you ask. She gives you a folder of seven color 5"x7" photographs. "Let me price it out," you respond. That means you are going to go back to your office and write out all the specs she has given you, plus add in some others that you know are givens. For example, you know that the finished size will have to conform to postal regulations, since this is to be a brochure that can be handed out or sent through the mail. When you have all the specs on paper, you will then contact vendors and subcontractors for prices on the various parts of the project that will have to be sent out, like typesetting and printing. Then you will figure out how much it will cost your agency in time and materials to produce those other parts of the project that will be done in-house. Once you have collected all of your prices, you will add them up and see how close they are to the client's budget. If the final total exceeds the budget figure of $5,500, then you will have to go back to the client and see what she is willing to cut back on. Maybe it could be the quantity she wants to print or the number of photos or the quality of paper.

If the total is less than the budget amount, then you tell her you can add options. What are those options? Options are design choices, like the number of colors you can have within that price range, or upgrading the quality of the paper the finished piece will be printed on, or adding illustrations or cartoons (if appropriate) to complement or supplement the photographs, etc. If, for instance, she chooses to add in another color, then you can reprice the job by finding out from the printer how much more an additional color would cost. You may continue putting in add-ons until the total budget figure has been reached. Or the client may decide to save some money and stay with the original price you gave her without the option of add-ons.

How to estimate a project

Let us use that same capabilities brochure as a sample project to illustrate how to break down the specs and estimate the cost to produce the job.

The first thing you do is break down the specs on a piece of paper. Most agencies will have spec sheets you can work from that will contain all or most of the information listed below. Then you will call any outside people you will need—vendors (printers, typesetters, etc.) and subcontractors (photographers, illustrators, other freelancers who might work on different parts of the job)—to give you prices for those aspects of the job that cannot be done in-house by your agency.

Project Specifications:

1. Budget: *$5500*

2. Elements needed to complete the job:
   - Design *yes*
   - Copy *no*
   - Mechanical Preparation *yes*
   - Typesetting *yes*
   - Photography *no*
   - Illustration *no*
   - Videography *no*
   - Printing *yes*
   - Delivery *no*
   - Mailing *no*
   - Other *no*

3. Costs for outside services:
   - Typesetting: $ *750.*
   - Printing: *2200.*
   - Veloxes: *210.*
   - Delivery: *95.*
   - Color Separations: *850.*
     Total: $ *4105.*

That leaves $1,395 for agency fees and materials. Now you have to figure out agency fees by determining the number of hours that will be spent on each aspect of the project. If you have not had much experience in pricing or you do not know how long things outside your area take to complete, you may have to go to other people on the staff to get their opinion of the time involved. Then you multiply the amount of time estimated by the hourly fee your agency charges for those services.

4. Cost for agency services:

• Design & Production:	Time	Cost
Layout	6 Hrs. x $60/Hr.	$ 360.
Copyfitting	2 Hrs. x $40/Hr.	80.
Mechanical Preparation	10 Hrs. x $40/Hr.	400.
Client Consultations	6 Hrs. x $60/Hr.	360.
Vendor Consultations	1.5 Hrs. x $60/Hr.	90.
	Total:	$ 1290.

Total Production Costs:	$ 4105.
Total Agency Fees:	1290.
Total Project Cost:	$ 5395.

That now leaves $105 remaining in the client's budget. It is better to stay under the budget than to price a project up to the limit. There are always changes that need to be made along the way that may run into extra money. So it is safer to keep a five to ten percent reserve in the budget, which this estimate does not allow for. So, in this case, you would need to go back into the estimate and see where you can bring the price down a bit.

From the agency's perspective, it is wiser to begin the cutback with printing prices than with agency fees. You have more room to cut back in the printing cost than anywhere else. You do not want to pare down agency fees because that can sacrifice quality. What that means is that if it takes an estimated eight hours to do a mechanical, you cannot decide to try and do it in six. Things like that cannot be done any faster without risking mistakes. Cutting back on the printing cost by eliminating one of the colors (if you are using more than one color to begin with, of course) or switching from a fairly expensive grade of paper to a house brand can save quite a bit of money without jeopardizing the final quality of the project. And the goal here is to produce the highest quality piece of work possible within the limitations of the client's budget.

An additional point to consider in your estimate may be sales tax. Your client might want that cost figured into the estimate as well. You may want to check with the client to see if that is a preference. Some clients just assume that tax will be additional. Personally, when I price out a job, I prefer to assume that sales tax will be additional. The reason for that is that estimating sales tax can be difficult since certain agency fees are taxable and others are not. And inevitably, project specs will change as a project progresses, and that will either increase agency time or decrease it. So rather than ask the client, I always include a disclaimer at the bottom of my price quotes that states that the total price does not include sales tax. That protects me and informs the client ahead of time. If the client wants the tax to be part of the budget total, that is the time to say so.

But most do not. I also incorporate into that disclaimer that this quote is an estimate only, and it does not include client requested revisions. That protects me from additional costs when clients begin making changes in the specs which alter the original quote.

How to get price quotes from vendors and subcontractors

It is standard procedure to get a price quote from three different vendors or subcontractors for each separate part of the job that needs a quote. If you need a price to print a job, you would ask three different printing companies to quote it and then compare their prices and choose the best one to include in your project estimate. The same thing is true for typesetting, color separators, photography, and any other parts of the job where it makes sense to compare competitors. The only time you would not bother with competitive bids is when an outside service like a particular illustrator or photographer has a unique style or quality that no one else can match.

To prepare your bid request, put together a spec sheet for each of the outside service people or vendors that outlines the details of the project portion that they will be responsible for. After they have their spec sheet, give them a specific period of time in which to get back to you with their price. The acceptable amount of time is about a week. If you need a quote really fast, like by the end of the day, say so. Most vendors or subcontractors can put something together if necessary. But do not make a habit of always asking for things right away.

The following is a sample spec sheet, to give you an idea of what information a printer would need to do a quote.

Printing Specifications

Project description:

Quantity to print:

No. of Pages:	Finished Size:	No. of Colors:
PMS Inks:	Screens:	Varnish:
Paper Stock:		No. of Photos:
Color Separations:		Bleeds:
Perforations:	Binding:	Delivery:

Other:

| Delivery Date: | Delivery Location: | |

If time permits, meet with each vendor or subcontractor individually and explain the job. If possible show them a mock-up. That way the vendors and subcontractors can make recommendations about certain things you may be able to do in the project that can save you considerable amounts of money. Or they may have creative ideas that can really enhance or complement your design. Do not forget it is a team effort, and the more input you get from others with experience in areas that are different from yours, the better the piece will be.

Get organized

Regardless of the job that you were hired to do in an agency, the two most important qualities you cannot survive without are organization and attention to details. The process involved in developing an advertising campaign, and then producing it and placing the ads in different types of media across the country, is highly complex and filled with minute details. If one detail such as an essential piece of information that has to be given to someone else is lost, overlooked, or left out, it can cost an agency hundreds or thousands or even millions of dollars. The pressure to keep track of all the details of even one campaign is almost mind-boggling, never mind the ten or twelve campaigns or projects any one person in an agency is working on at any given time. So being well organized and paying attention to every little detail is the only way you will survive in this detail-laden profession.

If organization and taking care of details is a weakness for you, then you may want to consider a time management class or some good books or tapes on the subject. If you are not a list maker who writes down everything you need to keep track of, become one. No matter how good your memory may be, the kind of trivial details you will have to remember in an agency will topple the best of you.

Do your best to learn whatever systems and procedures your agency has in place for taking a job from start to finish, tracking the progress of a job, and cost accounting. Any agency that has been around for a while will undoubtedly have its own system for doing things. Ask someone to explain to you, step by step, how a project moves through the agency. Every agency is different depending on its size and structure. Write down the steps and memorize them. I have included a general listing below to give you an idea of a sample system. When you are actually working in an agency, you may need to revise or change it completely.

THE FOLLOWING IS A GENERAL SYSTEM FOR MOVING A PROJECT THROUGH AN AGENCY.

1. The client meets with an agency account executive to explain the details of a project the client wants produced.

2. The A.E. then meets with agency management to get their approval to take on the project.

3. The A.E. meets with the traffic coordinator and the production coordinator to schedule the project and decide which agency staff people will work on it.

4. The A.E., the traffic coordinator, and production coordinator meet with the research department, media buyer and scheduler (if media is a part of the project), and the members of the creative team assigned to the project to discuss the details of the project and the schedule.

5. The research department takes a few days to do the necessary research. When that is complete, they meet again with the A.E., creative, and media teams to discuss the results and make recommendations about the direction the project should take or the slant it should have.

6. The creative and media teams (if media is involved) then begin their work. The creative people develop the concept of the project based on the research findings, and the media team develops a preliminary schedule and media cost proposal.

7. The creative team makes a presentation of the concept, preliminary sketches, and copy to the A.E. and management. The media team presents the schedule and cost proposal. The production coordinator also meets with the A.E. and management to present the production schedule and project price quotes. If all is approved at this point, the A.E. can present the work to the client for approval.

8. The A.E. meets with the client for approval of prices, schedule, concepts, sketches, copy, and media schedules and prices. The client approves, disapproves, or makes recommendations and changes.

9. After the A.E. meets with everyone who is assigned to the project to discuss the recommendations and changes the client made on the project, work begins to finalize designs, copy, details of the schedule, and prices.

10. The A.E. has another meeting with the client to get an approval on the finished designs and copy.

11. Production work begins—mechanicals, photography, photo shoots, and other subcontracting work.

12. The A.E. meets with management for approval of all mechanicals, commercials (if applicable to the project), schedules, prices, and last minute details. Then the A.E. meets with the client for final approval of all aspects of the project.

13. Mechanicals are delivered to the printer, ads and commercials to the media.

14. The client is billed.

Maintaining files

Be a fanatic about keeping separate files for each client and each project. Even if you have two or three projects for the same client, keep them in different file folders. Keep your files alphabetized and in order. There is never enough time when you work in an agency. You are always up against a deadline. If you have to take precious minutes away from doing a task while you are trying to locate important pieces of the job in a file that was just under your nose, you will find that minutes will turn into frustrating hours each week.

Keep a "to do today" list. Before you go home each night, cross off on your "to do" list everything that you did that day and add what you did not get to on your new list for the next day. Then straighten your desk and put everything in its proper place so that the next morning you can begin without facing a mountain of messy papers that have to be sorted through.

Reminding others

Never assume that anyone who is working on some part of a project that you are responsible for—especially vendors or subcontractors—will remember when their deadlines are and the details that they have to attend to. Always make a habit of calling your printer or typesetter to remind them that a deadline is approaching. If you have to deliver mechanicals for a job to a printer, make sure your salesperson is there to receive the job so that you can go over the details and specs and point out the due date. Include a written list of all the printing specifications on the mechanicals for your printer. You should do the same with your color separator by attaching a list of job specifications to the photos or chromes, and for your typesetter by attaching a layout of the design with the copy specified for size, type style, and fit. If you are involved with media, call your media representatives to remind them when a schedule or flight is about to begin.

It is not buggy if you are matter-of-fact in your tone and manner. Just tell them that you are calling to make sure everything is all set for such and such project. Your vendors and subcontractors have numerous projects for many different clients to keep track of. They will appreciate a thoughtful reminder, as long as it is not a reprimand or an assumption that they have forgotten.

Time sheets

An agency cannot exist for long without time sheets filled in by each employee every day. The one thing that most employees hate to do and forget to do is their time sheet. Nothing will irritate your boss faster than a time sheet that is blank, half filled in, or filled in on the basis of your memory at the end of the day, or worse yet, the end of the week. Why? Because a time sheet is your record of what you did for that day that is billable to a client for a specific project. Even though the agency has estimated ahead of time how long a particular project will take to complete, when it comes time to prepare the final bill to the client, the agency will go by the real hours put into the project. The only exception to this is if the hours put in exceed the estimate, and the additional hours do not reflect client requested changes that would have taken more time. In this case, the agency needs to know why a certain job took more time than estimated. That information will help them decide if they need to add in extra hours for a similar job on the next estimate. If they keep quoting jobs based on a projected amount of time that is not accurate, the agency will be losing money.

Time sheets are without a doubt a pain in the neck. They require that every time you begin work on a certain project that you grab that project's time sheet and log in your start time. Then you have to write down your activity, such as paste up or price quote, etc., and then log in the time you stopped working on that phase of the project. If you forget and try to go back at the end of the day, or as some people do, at the end of the week, there is no way you are going to remember exactly how much time you spent for each thing you did.

Agency production meetings

Most every agency has, at the very least, weekly production meetings with all members of the staff. During this time, management has the opportunity to get a report on the status of all projects. That includes what problems are occurring, how they are being handled and what is happening with new projects. Production meetings are an excellent time to see the entire agency in operation and understand how your work fits into that operation. This is also a great time to make yourself and your ideas visible to management. But do not try to steal the show. Use your thoughtful judgment as to when to speak up and when it is best to remain silent. Politics are strongly at work during agency production meetings. So be alert and take notes. The most important information you need to know about how to become an asset to your agency will be revealed during these meetings.

A look at the big picture

After you have been at the agency for several months, you should begin to get an idea of the big picture. What that means is, where is your agency going in terms of its goals, such as future growth, the clients it wants to attract, and the gross billings it is working toward in the future. If you are having trouble getting a clear picture of your agency's destination, make an appointment (wait at least six months or a year before you do this) with the agency owner. Then tell this person that you want to understand where the agency is headed so that you can help contribute to its goals. This will put you far ahead of most agency employees who only think about their own job responsibilities and never look to see how their work effects the growth of the agency. After the owner tells you, ask how you can help the agency achieve those goals. What recommendations would the owner give you as to the skills you should work on developing to their fullest, or any courses you can take to improve your work in the agency?

How reputations are made

An agency earns its reputation first and foremost by staying in business. As strange as that may sound, agencies come and go faster than any other business I have ever seen. The standard length of time a weak agency can stay afloat is about two years, then it begins to slowly or quickly sink from the horizon. I always maintained that a new agency opens up every month. It happens when some disgruntled employees leave and starts their own agency, convinced they can do it better. But few survive. Other agencies are born when a larger agency goes down and several employees who were cast adrift scoop up the handful of remaining clients and form a new agency. These are the agencies that usually make it. The prime candidates for failure are the know-it-all ex-employees who are fired or who quit; or investors who know nothing about advertising and buy a thriving agency, thinking they will pick up the tricks of the business as they go along. If they are lucky enough to keep on key employees and let them run the business, they may increase their chances of survival. But if they try to run the show themselves and do not recognize that they need to keep the experienced people on staff, and instead they try to save money by bringing in new, inexperienced people, that is a combination that spells certain disaster.

The second thing an agency builds a reputation on is ethical treatment of employees, clients, vendors, and subcontractors. That means charging reasonable prices, billing their clients fairly, paying bills on time, and treating people with respect.

Agencies also earn a reputation for quality work. Some agencies are good enough to produce work that is both high in quality and creative as well. These shops will become readily sought after by clients who like to brag about their agency and how many awards it has won this year. But these same clients are not usually the long-termers who will stay with an agency for years. Since having an agency that is in demand is important to them, they will usually leave when a new agency hits the trade magazines as a hot property.

How an agency makes money

Advertising agencies make money by charging their clients an hourly fee for their services. In addition to the fee, an agency places a markup on the price of all outside service work that is used, such as type, printing, photography, video production, etc., to complete a client's project. The markup varies with each agency, but the standard is 15 percent to 20 percent. Some agencies will charge as much as 30 percent to 50 percent. If they are asked to produce a rush job for a client (24 hour turnaround), it is not unusual for the agency to charge the client 100 percent markup on both agency fees and outside services. Along with fees and markup, an agency also earns a 15 percent commission from most media companies for the advertisements they place. So if an agency buys $10,000 in television time to run a client's commercials, the station that sold the time to the agency will give them a 15 percent discount off the total price of the purchase. That means that the agency will actually bill the client for the entire $10,000, but the agency will only have to pay the station $8,500.

Years ago, many advertising agencies were able to operate their businesses on commissions only. But the growing competition among media companies (newspapers, magazines, television, and radio) for a larger share of the advertising dollar caused many of them to eliminate commissions and begin charging agencies and direct clients the same discounted price. That decision opened a new market of business for the media companies from clients who no longer wanted to use advertising agencies, since it was now less expensive to place their own ads. In addition, these clients could hire a freelancer at half the price an agency would charge to produce their ads. A lot of agencies went under when this happened about fifteen years ago. The agencies that survived had to quickly restructure their pricing policies.

While some media companies were still offering discounted rates to agencies, the available client pool had thinned out, so agencies began to charge a fee for their creative and production services. Those fees today range anywhere from $50 to $200 an hour, or even more, depending on the location, size, and reputation of the agency. Few agencies charge a single rate across the board for all services. Their rates will vary depending on the service being performed. For instance, creative services may be billed at $120 an hour, layout and copy at $90. Mechanical preparation might be $60 an hour while clerical is only $35.

An agency operates on a profit margin of 1 percent to 10 percent, depending on how the agency is run and structured. So that means if an agency has a $100,000 account, the agency will end up with anywhere from $1,000 to $10,000 in its pocket as profit. The rest of the money will be spent on buying commercial advertising space and paying the agency for marketing advice, creative and production costs. It may sound like the agency will be making money on that, too, but that money paid to the agency from the client will be used to pay staff and operating expenses. The profit is what is left over when all the money has been spent to pay salaries and other expenses.

The question most often asked is how does an agency decide how much to charge for its fees. The agency does that by determining the total cost of its operating expenses. The operating expenses include rent, utilities, supplies, equipment, perks (cars, insurance, bonuses, commissions), furnishings and salaries. As an example, if an agency's total cost to operate its business is $20,000 a month, and we multiply that by 12 months, we get a figure of $240,000. That is the minimum amount of money that must be earned in a year by the agency to pay for its operating costs. Of course, that leaves no profit. From there, to figure out how much the agency must charge its clients to bring in the minimum necessary to pay its bills, we need to go back to the operating cost of $20,000 a month and divide that by 4 weeks a month. That comes out to $5,000, which is what the agency now has to bill in a week. Then we will need to divide the weekly amount by 5 days, which will give us $1,000 each day. In order to determine how much the agency must charge to earn $1,000 a day, we need to divide that by 8 hours, and we get an average hourly rate of $125 per hour. That now becomes the base figure the agency can work with to structure its fees.

Since most agencies have more than one person doing billable work in a day, the agency can use the top figure of $125 as the maximum amount it will charge a client for work that represents its most valuable services. Those services generally include client meetings with agency principals (other employees might be billed at a lower rate since they are not being paid as much), and creative concept development. Then design and copy work can be billed out at a lower rate. And other services such as mechanical preparation, subcontractor consultations, and clerical can be offered at an even lower rate. With three employees working at an average rate of $60 an hour, for 5.5 hours a day (the average amount of billable time an employee is usually able to clock in a given day), the agency can still earn $990 a day, which is close enough to our $1,000 minimum needed in a day.

So that gives the agency a fair amount of latitude within which it can structure its variable fee rates. And since an agency will also be charging markup on services and getting commissions for all the media it places, in addition to the $1,000 a day earned in fees, the agency will be earning more on top of that to enable it to realize a profit.

How do you fit in?

Once you get comfortable in your new agency, keep your eyes and mind open wide. By now you should have a good idea of how your work fits into the daily scheme of the agency's workflow, and how your work earns money for the agency. In addition to that, you also have to know who is who in the agency. You need to get a sense of who is important to the agency owner or owners, and why are they important? Also find out who is viewed as an insignificant employee. In other words, who is a pain to work with or ineffective? When you find out, stay away from these people. People on the outs at the agency will often begin indulging in negative talk and agency bashing. This can be very contagious. And you can be vulnerable to their influence, especially if you are still feeling new and looking for companionship. Agency management and owners watch these people carefully, usually for an excuse to let them go. If you are seen as one of their compatriots, you will not be long behind their exit.

Make a habit of associating with people you can learn from. Make that the basis of any friendships that develop early on in your employment. Later, once you know your territory and who you can trust and who you cannot, you can open yourself up for deeper friendships.

Make yourself invaluable

Whatever position you are in, whatever job you are given to do, do it to the best of your ability. Take pride in every little thing you do—no matter how small or seemingly unimportant. When you have some spare moments, look around and see what needs to be done or who you can help. Do not wait to be asked to pitch in. Make yourself invaluable to everyone around you. If you work in the art department, do not think that it is beneath you to lend someone from the clerical staff a helping hand by running errands or answering the phones when you have some extra time. They will appreciate your thoughtfulness, and word will get back to the people at the upper levels that you are ready to help anyone.

Never make a promise you cannot keep

It is far better to say no, with an explanation that you do not want to take on something that you cannot give your full attention to, than to take on too much work because you are afraid someone will get mad at you if you do not. If you do a poor job trying to hurry through it and still complete all your other work, you can be assured that the person who asked you to do it will be angry. And you may end up jeopardizing that person's job, if your work is what he or she has to show to a supervisor or a client is not top notch. That person will be held responsible, not you—at least for the time being. Sooner or later it will come back to you when you do a lousy job. And it will come back to you when you do a great job.

The office grapevine

Every office has a grapevine through which news—truth or rumors—will circulate. You cannot avoid it. If you begin to get wind of a story about you, whether it is truthful or not, try to locate the source and snuff it out at its root. How do you do that? Ask the first person you heard it from where he or she heard it, then go to that person and ask who the next source was. Keep following the rumor from source to source until you get back to the original mouthpiece; then ask that person what the rumor was based on. Do not approach this person with malice or anger. There is usually a grain of truth in every rumor. If there is, own up to what you did or said. Then square any hard feelings that may have occurred as a result of your actions. Then explain the real truth to your source person and get on with your work. Never let an untrue or half-true rumor or misconception hang around uncontested. It will always get worse. In the long and short run, it is always to your advantage to be honest and up-front in your communications and actions.

Never underestimate the power of office politics

Politics in an office environment means looking out for the welfare of one's self. Some people do this more than others. If you are going to survive and thrive in an agency, you have to be conscious of office politics and conform to it. In other words, watch out for yourself. Do not expect anyone else to do it for you. And never underestimate how powerful office politics can be in shaping your future with the agency.

There will always be people in an office who will try to use office politics in a shrewd or unethical way to put themselves in a better position with agency higher-ups or clients. Stay away from them. And also be aware of who they are, and that you can become one of their political pawns at any time. Be careful who you complain to, who you confide in, or cast jeering throw-away remarks to. These people will pick up any tidbit of information that can be used or twisted to make themselves look good and others, like you, look bad.

Partaking in office politics does not have to mean siding up to someone you do not like, just to get ahead. It means being nice to everyone in the office, not getting involved in gossip or sneaky behavior, and making an effort to be present at all office functions, even if you hate them. This is a necessary part of office comradery. Remember people's birthdays and anniversaries. Be a team player who is more concerned about the welfare of the agency and the client. Be loyal to your agency outside the office by holding all client and agency information that you are privilege to in complete confidentiality. The old military saying, "loose lips sink ships" is so true. And if you talk too much, the ship you sink will be your own.

Never take an office relationship for granted

Working in an ad agency office can soon become as comfortable and familiar as home. After all, you are there eight hours a day, sometimes more. And the people you work with can become like family members. And just like family, it is easy to brush off someone you work with or be abrupt or even rude, without intending to be. The people we are the closest to are the very people we pay the least amount of attention to when we are rushed, harried, or in a bad mood. We think that they will understand. And often they do. And that makes it all the easier to take them for granted.

But sometimes they do not understand. Sometimes their feelings get hurt, and they get angry. It is extremely important in a work environment to keep a close check on your temper, mood, and attitude toward others. Everyone in an agency is under constant pressure to meet deadlines and produce work that is highly taxing, physically and mentally. So if your temper flares, it will not take much to effect a co-worker. When this does happen in the office, try to catch yourself as soon as possible. Stop yourself and apologize before things get out of hand. The worse thing you can do is figure that the other person will get over it.

There will also be times when you may become so involved in your mood, plus absorbed with your work demands, that you may not even notice that you have offended someone. If you sense that a co-worker is acting strangely toward you, it is best to confront the situation directly and ask if there is a problem. If you have said or done something to upset this person, a sincere apology and an explanation of what was going on with you will set things right again. But if you stubbornly hold on to the belief that things ignored will disappear, in time you may be in for a real shock. In an office, when one person gets offended by your actions, that is only the beginning. In an effort to feel better, that person is going to tell other people. As soon as this hits the office grapevine, it will go straight to the ears of the agency owner(s), and you can be sure it will be greatly distorted by the time it gets there. An employer cannot afford to have a disrupter or troublemaker taking up precious agency time with people being upset and venting their anger through the only vehicle they have—their mouths. Having a bad reputation or unpredictable attitude, being moody or difficult to get along with, or simply ignoring common courtesy and taking people you work with for granted can be an express ticket to your exit.

Five magic words

It is nearly impossible to escape making a mistake when you work in an agency. Every time you touch something in the agency, there is a mistake waiting to happen. It is inevitable and unavoidable. Hopefully, if you are extremely careful, detail oriented, well organized, and alert, you can keep your mistakes to a minimum. But the plain fact is, sooner or later you will make one.

When this happens, if you discover it first, go immediately to an agency owner. Do not wait for someone else to find out about it. Then explain what happened, how it happened (if you know), and try to have a solution prepared to offer, if possible. If not, do not try to fake one. The main thing to remember when a mistake occurs, are the five magic words you can say that will keep you off the owner's black list. Those words are, "I'm sorry. It's my mistake."

I could never understand why people said that it takes a courageous person to admit a mistake. I think it takes more courage to hide it, because when you are found out, you are going to need all the courage you can muster to go out and find a new job, especially when you have to explain to an interviewer that you lost your last job because you made a mistake and did not own up to it.

Contrary to most people's opinions, a mistake is not an indication that you are incompetent, incapable, or just plain sloppy. A mistake will happen to everyone in your agency. It is part of being human to make mistakes. The greatest thing about them is that they are a wonderful opportunity to learn about yourself. If you can look at the mistake and ask yourself why it happened, you will discover an invaluable lesson.

Many people are afraid of owning up to a mistake for fear they will be criticized by others. But the fact is you will be more severely criticized if you are caught covering it up. When you come right out and admit that you were wrong or that you misjudged a situation or that you assumed something you should have checked on, other people will actually admire your candor, your honesty, and your ability to look squarely at yourself. In addition, your ability to freely admit your mistakes will allow others around you to feel more comfortable in admitting to their own shortcomings. In effect, your honesty and ability to admit your mistake can create an atmosphere in which people are not afraid to be vulnerable, knowing that they will be accepted, not condemned.

AFTERWORD

Ultimate success depends on you

Where are you going?

The time will come when you will finally be settled into your job and able to take the focus off learning how to survive in the agency. Now you can switch the focus to yourself and see exactly where you are going. Knowing where you are going is essential if you want to get somewhere. If you do not have a direction, then you end up just wandering around aimlessly. You may think that advertising is enough of a direction. But that is only your profession. Now you have to decide where you are going to go in the profession of advertising.

There are a lot of choices available to you. You could stay at the first agency you get a job with for the rest of your life and move up to positions of great responsibility. Or you could leave your first agency after a few years and get a higher level position at a bigger or more prestigious agency. You could even set your sights on getting as much experience as possible in an agency, or several agencies, and then opening an agency of your own. Or you could work for agencies as a freelancer. And another option is to leave agency work altogether and work in a corporate or nonprofit environment. You could also get out of the *doing* of advertising and go into the *teaching* of advertising.

This chapter will present the pros and cons of each of these options. It will also help you evaluate your own desires for your future, from a career perspective as well as a personal perspective. Then once you know where you want to go, you will learn how to develop an action plan that will get you there. Finally, you will find out why it is important to have a goal, but why it can be dangerous to fall in love with it.

Moving up, not out

If you are able to keep your job in the first agency that hires you for at least a year, you can begin thinking about moving up. Moving up may mean simply taking on more responsibility for—hopefully—more money, but not necessarily getting a new job title or a new job description. For example, if you were originally hired as a graphic designer, after a while you may be asked to expand your duties and do less designing and more supervising of the newer fledgling designers.

But the time may come when taking on more responsibility is not enough for you. You may want to move up into a higher position—a promotion with another job title and a higher salary. That opportunity might come to you strictly by chance, or you could begin laying the groundwork for that to happen within the first several months of employment with your new agency.

You certainly do not want to walk into an agency on the first day of work and already be thinking about a promotion. That could be a bit premature. But after a few months you should begin to sense whether or not this place feels comfortable to you. Do you like the people you are working with? Does the agency appear to be on solid ground financially? If so, then you may want to start thinking about carving out a future with this agency. How do you do that? By closely observing the people you work with. How many of the employees have been with the agency for at least five years? How many of them have been there longer? As you get to know your fellow workers better, you begin to get a real sense of just how happy they are in their positions at the agency. Keep your mind open as you learn what they like at the agency and what they do not. You may feel very positive about the agency for the first year and then, little by little, begin to see things that are not to your liking. After two or more years there you could begin to form a very different opinion about your desire for a long-term stay with the agency. The veterans of over five years will be your best guide about the true nature of the agency's wearability.

What determines this wearability? Probably the most important thing is how the owners treat the employees. Are they fair in their expectations? Are they generous financially in providing regular salary increases? How do they handle interoffice squabbles, disciplinary measures, and employee disputes? Do the employees feel appreciated when they pitch in and go that extra mile to help out? Do they feel like individuals who have valuable skills, talents, or abilities to contribute to the agency, or do they feel like hired help? Have the long-term employees stayed with the agency because they feel like it is a wonderful place to work and they want to be there? Or do they stay because they are scared they will have a hard time finding a comparable job elsewhere?

As for yourself, even if the agency does pass your many litmus tests of employee satisfaction and longevity, can you see an open track along which your career can continue to move and expand? If the agency is small, can you see a place within the agency's structure that would allow you to move up into not just one position of greater responsibility but several over many years or even a lifetime of advancement?

For example, suppose you were hired as an account coordinator to take care of the many details of client accounts. This is a nice entry level position that could keep you happily productive for a year or two. But where else could you move up within the agency after that? If the next position that you would like to move up to is an account supervisor, and the agency vice president, who is also one of the owners, is acting as the account supervisor, would that person have to leave before you could have an account supervisor's position? What are the chances that an owner would leave the agency? Practically nil! Are the owners interested in allowing the agency to grow enough to support another account supervisor? If not, and some small agencies are perfectly content to maintain a fixed number of accounts and employees, you may be stuck in a dead-end job. These are the questions you will need to consider about your agency.

As I mentioned in Step Eight, when you have been with the agency awhile (at least six months or a year), you would schedule an appointment with your boss (the agency owner or one of the owners) to talk about the agency's future goals and how you can help it achieve those goals. When you have had that meeting, you should have a much better sense of how you could fit into the agency in the future. You should ask your boss questions about potential agency growth. You also need to know what kind of clients the agency would like in the future, and how the staff will expand to meet those future demands. If you can see yourself fitting in with these plans, then you are ready to lay the groundwork for your next move up.

That groundwork involves doing the best job you can do each and every day. It also involves learning everything you can about the business of running an agency. Because moving up means taking on greater responsibility, so that one day you will cease to be a cog in the wheel of the agency and become the power that turns the wheel. Laying the groundwork includes spending your own time and money to get the outside training and education (if necessary) to take on that responsibility. That may mean taking courses to gain additional technical or management skills. It also means reading and learning all that you can about your niche or area of specialization, as well as advertising in general.

You may find that if you do have an area of specialization, such as graphic design or copy, and if you were hired to work exclusively in that area, you may at some point begin to feel that this area is not exactly what you want to do for the next five years. In that case, try to sense during your first year of employment what aspects of your job you love and what aspects you hate. What you love and hate will be very telling if you are trying to figure out what new speciality you should move to.

Here is one of the first clues that may tell you that you are not completely happy with your speciality. When you work with other people in the agency, do you ever find yourself envying what they are doing? Do you get fascinated by the work that comes out of the art department, and wish you could be sitting at a drawing board doing paste-ups and layouts or computer graphics? Whatever you find yourself drawn to, talk to the people who do it. Ask them what they had to study and learn to do their work. Then go for it. Take a course or two. And if you find that you not only have an interest or fascination in a particular area but an aptitude or talent for it as well, then give it your all.

Discuss your interest and the training you are pursuing with your employer. Be clear that, while you are happy in your present position, you are setting new goals to switch your area of specialization in agency work. You need to find out if your employer is supportive of your new career direction and if an opportunity might be available for you in the future to move into this kind of position. If the answer is no, then you should be honest and say that once you complete your training, you will be looking elsewhere. You also need to assure your employer that whether there will be another position for you at the agency or not, you will give your present job your full attention while preparing yourself for your career transition.

If you do see a pathway to a higher position that is clear and open to you in your present agency, make your intentions known to your employer. It is important to get feedback on how you could groom yourself for that job. It also gets your employer tuned in to your personal goals. If your employer is supportive of you, you could not only get some valuable advice and insight about how your goals fit in with the agency's, but also if this seems to be the right career direction for you.

If you decide to really commit to your present agency for the long haul, what are the chances of becoming a partner in the agency at some point in the future? And are you at all inclined in that direction? If you are, you have to find out whether the owner or owners are open to bringing on new partners. Some agency owners are just not willing to share their interest in the business. If you find out that the owners are open to accepting new partners, before you approach anyone, be sure you know them really well and that you would definitely consider a partnership option down the road. Also make sure that the owners respect you, trust you, and like you well enough to even consider you for a partnership. It is advisable to give yourself at least two years with an agency before you even begin to consider partnership.

A partnership is a very serious thing. It is like a marriage. All partners are fully responsible for each other, both financially and ethically. And partners must be able to depend on each other without doubt. Trust is essential. You must be ready to take on that kind of commitment before you consider it. Once you become a legal partner, you cannot just one day say you do not want to do it anymore. Partnerships are costly to get into and even more costly to get out of. When you are certain that this is a direction you would like to move in, bring the topic up privately. Keep the response you get strictly to yourself. Partnerships are only offered to a select few. And if you are ever lucky enough to be accepted, revere that honor and do not boast it around the office. It can cause resentment among the remaining employees who were not considered.

When a partnership is offered, it means you will have to buy into the agency. That could happen by offering you a certain number of shares in agency stock in lieu of a percentage of your salary. You should have your own attorney (not the agency's) represent you in the negotiations and in reviewing the details of the partnership contractual agreement. I would also strongly recommend that you take out partnership insurance. See if the agency already has such a policy and if you can buy into it. If not, urge your future partners to consider it. If they will not, you may still be able to get it on your own. Since legal partners are liable for the debts of any and all of the other partners, that could leave you in a sorry state if one of the partners skips out, leaving behind a mountain of bills no one knew about, or embezzles money from the firm. It can also be messy if a partner dies and the family tries to take over the deceased person's share in the company.

Setting your sights on other agencies

What if you find that you really do not want to stay at your first agency? Or that it would be a wise career move not to stay there? Then you have to start looking at other agencies. Just as you did to find a job in an agency the first time around, you will have to begin researching area agencies all over again because agencies can change drastically in just six months. If you are willing to move out of the area, you may want to expand your research into agencies in other locations. It all depends on what you want from another agency that you are not getting from your present agency.

The fortunate part is that you will have a basis of comparison once you have been with an agency long enough to evaluate whether it is the right one to commit to or not. If not, be sure you know exactly why. Is it too small and does not give you enough challenge in the kind of clients it handles? Or is it too small to allow you to move into higher levels of more responsibility? Is it so large that you feel like you are getting lost in the crowd? Is the atmosphere unsupportive, or is it stifling your growth or creativity? Knowing what you do not want and what you do want in your next agency will help you zero in on exactly the right place for you. Of course, you may not find out for sure if an agency is right for you just through your research. You will not know until you begin interviewing for the your next position.

Unless your present agency is really unbearable, do not change agencies just to make a lateral move into the same position. And do not take a cut in salary. Switching agencies and jobs becomes an important part of your career history. Future employers will wonder why you accepted less money. They might assume that you had a problem with your former agency. If it is at all possible, you want your resume to reflect upward movement and career progress. That means moving to another agency, taking on more responsibility and making more money, but with the same title as your previous job, ask your new employer-to-be to consider changing your job title. For instance, if you had the title of graphic designer at your last agency and are moving to a new agency as a graphic designer supervising other designers, ask if there is an art director. If there is and your new employer is resistant to having a second art director, ask if you could be given the title of assistant art director. If not, go for senior graphic designer or supervising designer or managing designer—anything that would appear to be a step up on your resume. And try to be just as conscientious with your salary, too. Even if it is only an increase of five hundred or a thousand dollars, be sure that you are going into a new job at a higher salary level than your previous job.

Leaving agency work completely

What do you do if you discover that working in an ad agency is just not where you want to be right now? Instead you find that your thoughts and interests are being drawn somewhere else. Perhaps one of the companies your agency handles holds greater attraction for you as a place to work than the agency does. Maybe you still want to do advertising, marketing, or design work, but you want to do it someplace other than an ad agency. Maybe you find yourself fascinated by the editing process each time you get to work on a client's television commercial in a video production studio. Or it could be that you cannot stop thinking about how terrific it would be to work in a college publications or public relations office. No matter what it is that you find yourself dreaming about, it is important to explore the feelings behind the dreams.

Working in an advertising agency is not for everyone. And if in spite of all your best efforts, you just cannot warm up to it, then it is time to begin exploring your options. Throughout this book I have spotlighted positions available outside of agency work. Take the time to go back through and read all of those Focus boxes again that talk about alternatives to agency work. The difficult part to accept when someone is going through the soul searching process of exploring alternatives is that many people begin to feel guilty. This is especially true if they have spent years going to school to earn a degree or certificate. But the fact is, for most people, it is not advertising they are rejecting or even their chosen speciality, it is the agency work that they are not suited to.

If you find yourself facing this kind of guilt, keep in mind that guilt is an albatross that will keep you stuck in place. Nothing can ever be accomplished when there is no movement forward. Forward movement in your career involves not only advancement upward, but also the motivation to become the best you can be for yourself. And that takes commitment, interest, excitement, and involvement in what you are doing each day. If you hate to come into work every day because the environment in an agency is a vexation to your spirit, but you love the work you do, then change your environment. If you can find a supportive and enjoyable environment that you love in a place other than an ad agency, that combination of loving where you are and loving what you do is exactly what you need to assure your future happiness and success.

Have you chosen the wrong speciality?

Maybe it is not the environment that is creating your sense of discontent. Maybe it is the work you are doing. If you got into research because you always scored high grades in reading comprehension and verbal communication, but you do not give a hoot about socioeconomic statistics or demographic breakdowns, then you had better look long and hard into your heart, not your head, for the answer to your dilemma.

It takes passion to succeed

Many people get into a certain career track simply because they are good at something, but that does not mean that they love it. If you do not love what you do, you cannot maintain your motivation and interest. Without motivation and interest, you are doomed to a life of career mediocrity. Your work will always be so-so, okay, good but not great. Great work requires inspiration born out of an intense, underlying excitement about what you are doing. And that kind of excitement and inspiration guarantees success.

Really successful people do not just appear successful, they feel successful. Not because of the money they earn or the car they drive or the clothes they wear, but because they know that inside of them burns an eternal flame of passion for their work. Their work is an extension of who they are as human beings. The two cannot be separated. And even if they could never earn another penny from the work that they love, they would hock everything they own just to be able to continue doing that work.

If you do not have this feeling of passion for your work, then stop using your head to figure out what you want to do. People who use their heads try to reason out what is best for them. These are the same people who think that what you do should be what you are good at. If you are one of those who falls into this way of thinking, you will always find yourself in that inevitable trap that keeps you doing what you are good at and never loving it. It is safe and comfortable, and you will never have to worry about failure. Of course, you will never achieve greatness, either. If you can stop using your head and go into your heart, you can get in touch with what feels right to you, rather than trying to think about what is right for you. You will find your passion right there in front of you, just waiting to be recognized.

It is not that you do not know what your passion is. You do. You have always known. It has been with you since you were a kid. But somewhere along the line you were told that you were good at something or had an aptitude for it, and that is what you assumed career decisions were based on. But think back to what you have always loved doing—the thing that could make you forget about time. Maybe you were totally fascinated with motion pictures as a kid and pestered your parents for a Kodak movie camera. Then you begged and borrowed to buy an 8mm editing machine and had a great time stringing family movies together and matching them up to a sound track that you taped on your cassette recorder. And now since working in an ad agency as a designer, the thing you love most is when you develop a storyboard for a television commercial and direct the videography and editing. That is when you notice that you could spend all day in a video editing studio. It is a thrill. But then it is time to be back to the same old thing at the agency, drawing up layouts and specing type. Ho hum. It never occurs to you that what makes your heart sing with joy is what you could be doing for a living.

"Me," you say: "I can't be a video editor. I went to school for years to become a graphic designer. I know practically nothing about editing or operating all that computer equipment. You can't just decide overnight to change your career direction and become a video editor. And you don't just walk into a video production house and say, 'Guess what, I want to work here.'"

Well, the fact is that you *can* decide to be a video editor overnight, if your heart tells you that is where your passion lies. And you are right, you cannot just walk into a video production house and say you want to work there—at least not if you expect to get paid. But you can ask to do an apprenticeship there and work with an editor to learn how to do that job. And what better preparation could you have for that job than your four years of graphic design background and your ad agency experience with storyboards, clients, campaigns and advertising theory? You can keep your regular job with the agency while you work weekends or nights at the production company learning the ropes. When you are ready, there just may be a job for you with that company. Or at the very least, you will have a demo reel put together to take to other production houses or television stations. And I guarantee that your first job offer as a video editor will not be far behind.

So follow what your heart is trying to tell you the next time you find yourself totally enthralled with something you are doing. Do not place limitations on yourself by deciding in advance that something is not possible. When you explore all the options, you will find that what seemed impossible at first glance was limited only by your narrow point of view. Broaden your point of view and you expand your possibilities.

Going it alone

After you have been with an agency for a while, you may just find yourself thinking that you could be happier as a freelancer working for agencies. But what are the tradeoffs? As you watch the freelancers come and go in your agency, you may find yourself envying the freedom they have and the work they get to do. It may look like a great life to you. No nine to five routine, but still all the fun and excitement that advertising has to offer. And the money they seem to make is not bad, either. Some of them are making $50, $60, or $70 an hour. But what is the real story? Let us compare working as a footloose freelancer to working as a full-time agency employee.

A freelancer takes in work from agencies on a per project basis and usually gets paid by the hour. The nice thing about freelancing is that if you are good and are able to build up a steady base of agencies, you can make a decent amount of money. It does, however, take time to get to that point, so you should count on a backup source of income while you are getting started. When freelancers have a good reputation and their services are in demand, they can begin to increase their hourly rates. When higher hourly rates are combined with the advantage of low overhead (a studio in their homes), freelancers really begin to see the profits roll in.

Freelancers have a lot of independence because they do not have to keep their offices open during set business hours. An answering machine is all they need to let them know when clients call. And they do not have to worry about asking a boss when they can take an afternoon off or a week's vacation.

The downside of that is if a freelancer becomes too independent, by turning work down too frequently, agencies will turn to other freelancers when a job needs to be done. There are always others willing to do the job cheaper or quicker. They may not be as good, but that does not always matter. What does matter is that agency people are constantly under the gun to stay on schedule. If a freelancer disappoints them once and they can find a convenient replacement, they probably will not use that unreliable freelancer again.

Freelancers are self-employed, and as such they are responsible for keeping an accurate record of all the money they make and reporting it to the IRS at the end of the year. For every job they take in and bill, they should keep aside a certain percentage to pay their income taxes. In addition, they have to charge their clients sales tax for some of the work that they do if they live in a state with a sales tax. And it is entirely their responsibility to know what the laws are that determine when they should charge sales tax. They also have to keep careful records of all client work and income. They must files a sales tax statement every month, even if they have not performed any work that is taxable or earned any income that month. Freelancers can save themselves aggravation, not to mention expensive penalties, if they consult an accountant early on to help them set up their books, advise them about sales taxes and filing their state and federal income tax returns. Freelancers have to make provisions for their own health insurance. While retirement plans and income disability insurance are not an absolute necessity, it is a good idea for the serious freelancer to investigate the many options available.

One last comment about freelancers is that they are usually thought of by most people in the business community (especially those who are asked to extend them credit), as well as their parents and even their friends, as being less than serious about working. They are always asked, "So, when are you going to settle down and get a real job?" When the freelancer tries to explain that freelancing *is* a real job, these same people will then ask, "And what is it exactly that you do for a living?" It can be frustrating, and the truth is a freelancer may never be taken seriously until there are advertising awards all over the walls, and newspaper reviews of professional accomplishments are in every critic's hand.

If after reading this, being a freelancer seems too hard or too frightening to even think about, then you probably want to stay with a full-time position. There you can concentrate all your time and energy learning to be the best that you can be in your chosen area. You will not have to worry about where the next project or your next paycheck will come from. You will be free of worry about saving enough money to pay your self-employment income taxes at the end of the year. You will probably have a nice health and benefits package, including paid vacation time, set aside for you.

Switching from *doing* to *teaching* advertising

I never believed the expression, "Those who can do, and those who can't teach." To be a good teacher, you have to know how to do whatever it is that you are going to teach. After you have been working in advertising for several years and you have a solid understanding of how the business works and exactly what one must know to create effective advertisements, you may want to consider sharing your knowledge and skills in a classroom.

This can be done while you are still working in advertising if you teach adult education courses. Many local colleges and high schools offer continuing education programs with classes in the evenings and on weekends. Or the day may come when you will decide that you have had enough of agency work and would like to do something that is not filled with deadlines and pressures. Teaching advertising full-time at a college can be a wonderful alternative.

Usually a master's degree is required for college level teaching. But when the subject matter deals with an area that can only be taught by someone whose expertise comes from years of actually working in the field, then practical hands-on experience will be accepted in lieu of the degree. Colleges that offer programs in advertising, marketing, communications, and design are always looking for competent professionals who can teach the many facets of these areas. So whether your niche in advertising happens to be design, production, copy, research, media, or account work, there will be teaching opportunities waiting for you if the time arrives when you would like to explore a totally different kind of environment in which to share your love of advertising.

Knowing yourself

The most important thing you can do for yourself is to stay in touch with that inner voice that comes from your heart, not your head. That voice will always tell you precisely what you want in your life. Knowing what you want and going after it is the key to inner peace and joy.

Most people have no clue about what they want in life. They spend the majority of their time pursuing goals that ultimately mean nothing to them. They may think these goals are important while they are chasing after them, but the feeling of importance comes not from the goal but the excitement of the chase. Once the goal is attained, there is a deep feeling of emptiness, an overwhelming sense of, "Now what do I do?" And the only answer to that question is to set another goal and to start the chase all over again.

If you have ever found yourself in that place where you were always setting goals, only to be left unfulfilled when you attained them, you were not in touch with what you truly wanted. Instead you were going after something you thought you wanted—a message delivered by your head, not your heart.

Your heads talks to you all the time. In fact, it chatters. It tells you what you *should do*, what you *could do*, and what you *would do* if only things were. . . . Your head logically reasons everything out trying to determine just the right move. It is also where you store your measuring stick—that instrument you use to measure your accomplishments, your successes, and your shortcomings against everyone else around you. The problem with that is that you are the one who will always come up short. There will always be someone out there who is smarter than you, better than you, more accomplished, and more successful. As a result, you will endlessly chase after a thing called "success," using other people as your model. And just when you think you have got it, a newer, better, and more current model will come along. And then the chase begins all over again.

After years of running in pursuit of a goal that you could never reach, if you are lucky, you will be one of the few who suddenly realizes that the goal—the model of success you were trying to become—had nothing to do with you. It had to do with everyone else around you and what they said they wanted. And your head, being the dutiful little recorder of the information floating around you, picked up their messages and fed them right back to you. You mistakenly took that information and believed it to be your own inner voice. It was an inner voice alright, but it was simply a recording of everything your head had ever heard that made logical sense. And that recording played over and over until you thought it was your own.

Once you recognize that you have been pursuing goals and desires set by other people—your parents, your teachers, your friends, and all the nameless faces you have seen on television shows and in advertisements, you will begin to see that you have been running on a treadmill that was leading nowhere. But you can make the choice to get off. Once you do, a strange unfamiliar silence will surround you. You will no longer be hearing the mindless roar of that ever-spinning treadmill. And in that silence, perhaps for the first time, you will hear a tiny, whispering voice that will deliver a message so powerful that you will wonder why you never heard it before. That message will give you the inner vision that will enable you to see through the fallacy of the beliefs you have been accepting as truth from your head for so many years.

That whispering voice is your heart. It comes from the feeling center of your body, not the thinking center. And knowing what you want in life can only be understood when you are in touch with your feelings.

Get in touch with your heart voice

The reason we all have so much trouble hearing that heart voice is because we have to be very quiet and still. We have to be outside our brain's chatter and the roar of the treadmill. You can get there through a variety of routes. Meditation is the most effective and direct way to tap into that heart voice. It does not even have to be any kind of formalized or ritualized meditation practice. It can simply be a time during each day when you just sit quietly and allow your head voice to slowly shut off, and in the remaining silence you will hear the whisper of your heart. It will tell you what is truly important to you alone. It will tell you how you really feel about your life, your work, and where you are going in your future.

And when you hear those messages from deep inside your heart, you will not have any doubt that they are the truth—your truth. You can also get in touch with your heart voice in other ways—sitting alone on the beach, jogging or walking, listening to music, drawing, or writing. It does not matter what you do, as long as it helps you disconnect from your chattering head and the thinking mode, and gets you into a feeling mode.

Setting your destination, developing a plan

Once you know what you really want, you will have a destination—a place you are heading toward. From that destination point, you can see clearly what direction you have to take from where you are now to get there. That direction becomes your path. Now you can develop an action plan made up of a series of goals that will move you along your path. These goals should be a series of small steps that are easily attainable. When you combine these steps together, they will become your plan of action.

To develop a plan of action, take a piece of paper and write at the top of it exactly what you are doing at the time you begin your plan. (For example, if you are working in an agency as a junior graphic designer doing paste-ups and layouts, then you would write that down.) That becomes your starting point. Then at the bottom of the paper, write down what you want to accomplish. (Maybe it would be that you want to leave the agency in several years and start your own freelance design business.) That now becomes your destination. Now go back to your starting point; beneath that, write down a brief description of what you will need in experience and knowledge to reach your destination. (That might be something like this: In order to attain the goal of having my own freelance business, I would need to work at the agency long enough to become an experienced designer and production manager with a thorough understanding of how an agency is run as a business.) After you have established that criteria, ask yourself this question: What action can I take today that will help move me closer to my destination? Remember this should be a small step that is easily accomplished. You do not want to overwhelm yourself anywhere along the way. When you have the answer to that, write it down and label it Action #1. (That might be: I am going to take a course in how to start a small business.) Then visualize yourself having completed that goal or action step. After that, ask yourself this question: Now that I have completed that goal, what is the next logical step that I should take to bring me closer to my destination? When you have that answer, label it Action #2. You will keep going in this manner, asking yourself the same question, and numbering each answer as an action until you arrive at the point where the next step is the destination itself.

Plans can change, so can you

You may find that some of the actions you take along the way will bring you to a plateau stage. When you arrive at a plateau, you will need to evaluate where you are now, and if you still want to continue moving toward your original destination. You may change your mind as you begin working toward your destination. And it is important to allow that to happen. You do not want to get so locked into where you are going that you do not see the other opportunities that may come along.

Look at your plan daily

When you have a written plan, look at it every day. Pin it up on the wall in front of your desk or tape it to your bathroom mirror. Having it in front of you will be a conscious reminder that will keep your mind focused on your destination. In addition, just seeing it there, even if you do not get a chance to read it each day, will allow your subconscious mind to act on bringing new ideas into your conscious awareness that will help you improve upon your action plan. Looking at it frequently will also keep you aware of those plateau stages when you hit them and if you need to alter your destination or change it altogether.

Your personal life versus your career life

Many people make the big mistake of getting so caught up in their careers that they forget about their personal lives. I did that for a while. My life became my work. I had lost who I was as a person. That was mostly because I never learned to listen to my heart voice, so I never knew what I really wanted. I chased after other people's idea of success for a lot of years. I had become a combination of all those people I thought I wanted to be like. When I finally stopped running the race to nowhere, I realized just how much I had shut off my feelings and shut out my family and friends.

This is the danger that awaits anyone who is embarking on a new career, especially a career in advertising. Because advertising is so demanding, it is easy to get totally enmeshed in it. So when you know what you want and decide on your destination, think about how it will impact your personal life.

I once knew a woman who began her career working in a mid-sized local agency. She went from being a paste-up artist to an art director in three years. She loved her work and was very good at it. Then she decided that she was not being challenged enough. She wanted the thrill and excitement of working on big, national ad campaigns and million dollar commercials. She knew that she would have to go to Boston or New York for those accounts. So she opted for Boston. She got a job with a big agency and was delighted. At last her career would get off the ground.

Then I heard from her about eight months later. She was miserable. "Advertising wasn't fun anymore," she said. The pressure in an agency of this size was unbearable for her. "When you're working on multi-million dollar projects, one little mistake, one little oversight could cost the agency hundreds of thousands of dollars," she told me. She also said that she could not sleep at night, her fiance broke off their engagement because he thought she was married to her job, and her doctor told her she had an ulcer. So be careful what you want and what you wish for. Sometimes the best of all possible worlds is right in your own backyard.

You are on your own

You have now come to the end of the book. I have shared with you everything I know about how to get a job in advertising and how to keep it. One last little bit of advice that I would like to pass along to you is something that I read when I was first starting out. It is called the Golden Rule of Success: *Do not do unto others as you would have them do unto you.* It took a long time for me to understand exactly what that expression meant, but now I finally understand it. It means that how you may want to be treated by others is not necessarily how other people want to be treated by you.

We often make the mistake of thinking we are doing something wonderful for someone—an unrequested good deed—only to discover that all our efforts went unappreciated. In fact, sometimes our efforts were downright scorned at by the recipient. Why, we wonder? And then off we go in a huff thinking that people are so ungrateful. This happens not only with friends and family but also with co-workers and bosses. We want to help them out, be supportive, do nice things. But then it backfires. They think we are butting in or being presumptuous. Before you take the initiative to lend a helping hand to a co-worker or boss or business associate, save yourself some aggravation and ask if that person would like to have that done. Ask if that is something that would help, or if there is something else you could do instead.

Remembering this simple golden rule will keep you in harmony with those around you at the office and out in the business community where friends often try to help each other. In the end, I think you will find that true success is measured by not only the quality of your relationship with yourself, but your relationship with others.

BIBLIOGRAPHY

Books

Stephen Baker, *Systematic Approach to Advertising Creativity*, McGraw-Hill, New York, 1979.

Diane Barthel, *Putting on Appearances: Gender and Advertising*, Temple University Press, Philadelphia, 1988.

Alec Benn, *The 27 Most Common Mistakes in Advertising*, 1st AMA Com., New York, 1981.

Edmond A. Bruneau, *Rx for Advertising*, Boston Books, Spokane, WA, 1986.

Ed. Caffery, *So You Want to Be in Advertising: A Guide to Success, What to Study, How to Prepare, What to do Once You're There*, Simon & Schuster, New York, 1988.

John Caples, *Tested Advertising Methods*, Prentice-Hall, Englewood Cliffs, NJ, 1974.

Eric Clark, *The Want Makers: Lifting the Lid off the Advertising Industry: How they make you buy*, Viking, New York, 1989.

George T. Clarke, *Opportunities in Advertising Careers*, Educational Books Division of Universal Publishing and Distributing Corp., New York, 1968.

E. L. Deckinger, *Exploring Careers in Advertising*, Rosen Publishing Group, New York, 1985.

Kenton W. Elderkin, *How to Get Interviews from Job Ads*, Elderkin Associates, Dedham, MA, 1989.

Jack Engel, *Advertising, The Process and Practice*, McGraw-Hill, New York, 1980.

Editors of *Fortune*, *The Amazing Advertising Business*, Simon & Schuster, 1957.

Jan Greenburg, *Advertising Careers: How Advertising Works and the People Who Make it Happen*, Holt, New York, 1987.

Robert William Jones, *The Business of Advertising*, Longman, London, 1974.

Judith A. Katz, *The Ad Game: A Complete Guide to Careers in Advertising, Marketing and Related Areas*, Barnes & Noble Books, New York, 1984.

Frank Kirkpatrick, *How to Get the Right Job in Advertising*, Contemporary Books, Chicago, 1982.

David Laskin, *Getting into Advertising*, Ballantine Books, New York, 1986.

Arthur W. Lavidge, *A Common Sense Guide to Professional Advertising*, Tab Books, Blue Ridge Summit, PA, 1973.

John Lyons, *Guts: Advertising from the Inside Out*, American Management Association, New York, 1987.

Jane Maas, *Adventures of an Advertising Woman*, St. Martin's Press, New York, 1986.

Nancy Millman, *Emperors of Adland: Inside the Advertising Revolution*, Warner Books, New York, 1988.

David Ogilvy, *Confessions of an Advertising Man*, Atheneum, New York, 1963.

David Ogilvy, *Ogilvy on Advertising*, Crown, New York, 1983.

David Ogilvy, *The Unpublished David Ogilvy*, Crown, New York, 1987.

S. William Pattis, *Opportunities in Advertising*, National Textbook Company, Lincolnwood, IL, 1988.

Annual Publications

Advertising Career Directory, Career Publishing Corp., New York, © 1985–1986.

Career Press, Hawthorn, NJ, 1987–annual.

Adweek, Agency Directory [New England Edition], A/S/M Communications.

RECOMMENDED REFERENCES

Books

Feel the Fear and Do It Anyway, Susan Jeffers, Ph.D., Fawcett Columbine, New York.

Key to Yourself, Venice Bloodworth, DeVorss & Co.

Giving in to Get Your Way, Terry Dobson and Victor Miller, Delacorte Press, New York.

Moneylove, Jerry Gilles, Warner Books.

Success Through a Positive Mental Attitude, Napoleon Hill and Clement Stone, Pocket Books, New York.

You Can If You Think You Can, Norman Vincent Peale, Fawcett Crest Books.

The Sky's the Limit, Wayne Dyer, Ph.D., Pocket Books, New York.

Take This Job and Love It, Dennis Jaffee, Ph.D. and Cynthia D. Scott, Ph.D.

Audio Cassettes

"Choosing Your Own Greatness," Wayne Dyer, Ph.D., Nightingale-Conant Corp., Chicago, Illinois, 1-800-323-5552.

"The Psychology of Success," Brian Tracy, Nightingale-Conant Corp., Chicago, Illinois, 1-800-323-5552.

"Getting Things Done," Ed Bliss, Career Track, Boulder, Colorado, 1-800-334-1018.

"Effective Listening Skills," Ron Meiss, Career Track, Boulder, Colorado, 1-800-334-1018.

"Project Management," Larry Johnson, Career Track, Boulder, Colorado, 1-800-334-1018.

"The Balancing Act," Bee Epstein, Ph.D., Career Track, Boulder, Colorado, 1-800-334-1018.

"How to Deal with Difficult People," Dr. Rick Brinkman and Dr. Rick Kirschner, Career Track, Boulder, Colorado, 1-800-334-1018.

"Negotiate Like the Pros," John Patrick Dolan, Career Track, Boulder, Colorado, 1-800-334-1018.

"Business Writing Skills," Debra Smith, Career Track, Boulder, Colorado, 1-800-334-1018.